Sport and Adventure in the Indian Jungle

Owing to the antiquity and rarity of this book, certain pages are regrettably absent, and readability is compromised due to the blurring of the original text. If you possess any insights regarding the availability of these missing sections, kindly inform us. Your assistance is crucial in ensuring the completion of this significant work for the benefit of future generations.

Sport and Adventure in the Indian Jungle

BY

A. MERVYN SMITH

GYAN

Published by

GYAN

Gyan Publishing House
5, Ansari Road
Daryaganj, New Delhi-110002
Phone: 011-47034999, 9811692060
E-mail: books@gyanbooks.com

Distribution Network
gyanbooks.com
India, USA, Canada, UK, Australia

ISBN: 978-93-6433-085-5 (HB)
First Published, 1904

2nd Impression 2024

Printed at: Gyan Press, Delhi.

SPORT AND ADVENTURE IN THE INDIAN JUNGLE
Author: A. MERVYN SMITH

Sport and Adventure in the Indian Jungle

TROPHIES OF A SIX-WEEKS' SHOOT IN HYDERABAD BY SOME OFFICERS OF THE 4TH HUSSARS.

Sport and Adventure in the Indian Jungle

BY

A. MERVYN SMITH

With Illustrations from Original Drawings and Photographs

LONDON
HURST AND BLACKETT, LIMITED
13, GREAT MARLBOROUGH STREET, W
1904

PREFACE.

The following stories originally appeared in the columns of the Calcutta *Statesman*, and are reproduced in their present form with the permission of the proprietors of that journal.

Most of the incidents narrated fell within the personal experience of the writer, much of whose professional life was spent in the jungle tracts of India. Where his description of the habits of wild beasts differs from that of accepted authorities, he can only plead that he has recorded the facts as they appeared to him at the time of their occurrence, and that he does not pretend to a scientific knowledge of the Indian *fauna*.

A. MERVYN SMITH.

LONDON, *March*, 1904.

CONTENTS.

SPORT AND ADVENTURE IN THE INDIAN JUNGLE.

AT THE *KHEDDAHS* WITH THE DUKE OF CLARENCE.

ALL Mysore was agog when it was known that the Heir-presumptive of the mighty Empire of the Kaiser-i-Hind was to visit that province. What sort of a reception should we give him? Was it to be the usual review of troops in garrison, triumphal arches, fireworks, and illuminations, the reiteration of sights which must have palled on him long ere he reached far-off Mysore? It was a happy thought indeed which fixed on a hunt of the leviathans of the forest as worthy the attention of our illustrious visitor. Sanderson, the *hathee* (elephant) king, was amongst us. He had just returned from his big catch of six hundred elephants in one lot on the Garo hills, and was now in charge of the *kheddah*, or elephant-catching operations, in Mysore. To him was entrusted the task of arranging a drive and capturing a herd of wild elephants in the presence of the Royal Duke. The Mysore table-land is almost denuded of jungle in the east, north, and centre. Along its western and southern borders primeval forests clothe the deep valleys of the Shayadri or Neilgherry mountains, and in this canopy of green, herds of wild elephants have disported themselves unmolested, from time immemorial. The Belligherry Rungan hills form an outlying mass of the Neilgherries, on the south-eastern frontier of Mysore, and, rising to a height of nearly five thousand feet, are clad with dense vegetation. Save for a solitary planter who had made a home in these solitudes, they were thus far untouched by the ruthless hand of the coffee-planter. Here was the favourite feeding-ground of numerous herds of elephants; and here was the spot chosen for the great "drive" to be witnessed by the grandson of our Queen.

Mysore's first glimpse of its illustrious visitor so shocked its anticipations of the Royal advent, that I am tempted to describe it. It was on a cold, misty morning in November that the special train conveying his Royal Highness steamed into the Pettah station. All official Bangalore and a large sprinkling of the native population were assembled there to do him honour, although his stay was to be for only a few minutes on the way to the capital and thence to the scene of the elephant-hunt. The train drew up, and all was expectation to catch a glimpse of the Prince. My native friends expected to see a personage decked out in cloth of gold and resplendent with jewels of inestimable value, such as they were accustomed to see among their own rajas; or at least a gorgeous uniform with cocked hat and feathers, and breast blazing with orders; and it took a good deal to convince them that the tall, slight figure which after some delay emerged from a saloon carriage, dressed in a pink silk night-suit, with naked feet thrust into slippers, and bare head, and alighted on the platform rubbing his sleep-heavy eyes, was the Royal visitor! The Prince had been asleep, and was awakened to have his cup of early tea. After he had partaken of this beverage, however, the Dewan (Chief Minister) of Mysore, Sir Sheshadri Iyer, and one or two others were presented to him. "What," said a native friend, "can this be his Royal Highness? No *chobdars* (silence-keepers), no mace-bearers, no guards, no standards, no firing of guns, nothing to distinguish him from the common?"

The *kheddahs*, or elephant-traps, were constructed in a heavily-wooded valley at the foot of the Belligherry Rungan hills, fifty-six miles from the railway terminus at Mysore city. For fifty miles the Maharaja of Mysore—a skilful whip—drove his illustrious guest in his four-in-hand up to the edge of the forest, whence saddle horses conveyed the party to the platform overlooking the massive drop-gate which was to close the entrance of the *kheddah*, once the herd of elephants had been driven into it. The *kheddah* had been constructed months before. A short description of this elephant-trap may not be uninteresting. During the dry months from January to May, when fodder is scarce on the plains, the elephants retire to the upper slopes of the hills, where green food is more abundant. With the first rains in June the herds seek the rich pastures at the foot of the hills, and make occasional raids into the neighbouring grain fields. During the absence of the elephants (from January to May) a site for the trap is selected at the foot of the hills, in some low, heavily-wooded valley known to be one of their favourite resorts. Plenty of forage, such as they love, and an ample supply of water are the great desiderata, and a ploughing or two, and planting with coarse cereals make the locality chosen more enticing. Three circular stockades, the largest one hundred and fifty acres in extent, the next one acre, and the smallest half an acre, with an opening from the largest into the second, and from that into the third, and all surrounded by a ditch eight feet deep and six feet wide, form the *kheddah*. Diverging lines of stockade and trench radiate from the circumference of the largest enclosure, and stretch across the width of the valley. When the herds come down from the hills and enter the top of the valley they gradually feed towards the lower end, till stopped by the diverging trench and turned towards the opening of the largest enclosure. Once within this enclosure the herd is practically secured, the entrance being guarded by a line of beaters, who frighten away the animals should they make any attempt to return. Here the elephants may be left till such time as it is convenient to begin the drive into the second or securing stockade. This large enclosure must be plentifully supplied with food and water, so that the beasts may not be in want of either during the time they are kept within the encircling stockade.

It was at this stage of the proceedings that the Prince and his party arrived on the scene to witness the drive into the second or securing stockade. Platforms high up among the branches of the trees, and overlooking the trap-door closing the entrance to the second enclosure, had been erected for the spectators, and to these the party was silently conducted. A cord connected with the arrangement for closing the great doors was placed in the hand of the Prince, and he was requested to give it a slight tug as soon as the last of the herd had passed from the first into the second enclosure. A herd of thirty-seven elephants had been quietly enticed into the largest enclosure about a fortnight before, and now at a preconcerted signal the drive was to begin. Boomay Gowda, the famous Sholigay tracker, of whom Sanderson gives an interesting account in his "Thirteen Years Among the Wild Beasts of India," had charge of this delicate operation. Beaters had been placed at intervals of thirty paces all round the large enclosure. These men were concealed from view, but should an elephant attempt to break through the stockade they would come out of their concealment, and the elephant, catching sight of them, would at once turn away. The beat was conducted in perfect silence, the spectators being asked to keep as quiet as possible.

We were told the drive had begun, but there were no signs of it to our uninitiated ears. The herd was being gradually worked in our direction; the beaters would flit from tree to tree, and the keen scent of the elephants would indicate the direction from which their human foes were approaching, and send them off in the opposite direction. It took fully an hour to drive the beasts half-a-mile and bring them within view of the platforms. When I first caught sight of them they were packed close together like a herd of swine. Some of the larger ones were evidently alarmed, and with trunks uplifted were endeavouring to scent on which side the danger lay. The younger ones—and there seemed to be several baby elephants among their number—were disporting themselves and chasing one another under the bodies and between the legs of their seniors. Browsing as they went, the herd gradually approached the trap-door. A young tusker was the first to enter; then followed some of the younger ones. Two large females, with very young calves at their heels, seemed instinctively to know that there was danger beyond the narrow opening, and would not approach the entrance, although the remainder of the herd had passed through. It looked as if they would have to be left out, and the trap-door closed, lest the others should return to the outer enclosure and rejoin the wary females. At this point the forest craft of Boomay Gowda came into play. The short yap of the wild dog was heard in the distance. Instinctively the little calves took shelter under

THE DUKE OF CLARENCE RETURNING FROM THE ELEPHANT KHEDDAH.

[*To face page* 7.

their mothers, while these latter turned anxiously in the direction of the sound. Another and apparently nearer yap settled the matter, and the anxious mothers, forgetful of the danger in front and only mindful of the foe behind, set off to join the herd and passed through the gates, which closed with a bang. A hurrah from the spectators sent the whole herd flying to the far end of the second enclosure, and through that into the third. This ended the first day's drive. It should here be mentioned that the second enclosure is cleared of underwood and small trees; only the large trees are allowed to stand, and to these the elephants are secured when captured. The third enclosure is completely bared of trees and brushwood. Just before the drive, large bamboos, with all their branches and leaves on, are stuck firmly in the ground to resemble a bamboo forest. The frightened elephants rush eagerly into this cover, and remain concealed in it while the door is being secured. Watchers encircle the stockade, and there the animals remain till next day, when the more exciting operation of singling out and securing each member of the herd begins.

A fine camp of some thirty-two tents, pitched in open ground, three miles away from the trap, afforded accommodation for the night to the *shikar* party. After an early breakfast, we were off to the *kheddahs* to witness the lassoing and securing of the elephants. On arriving at the platform overlooking the third or smallest enclosure, what a strange sight met our gaze! During the night the elephants had trodden down all the artificial shelter of bamboo trees, and were now grouped together in the centre, sterns inwards, and heads facing the circle of stockade. The previous evening they had entered with skins black and glossy, and with all the pride of independence in their gait ; now mud-bespattered, disreputable, and cowed, they looked exactly like a herd of swine awaiting slaughter. The squeal of the baby elephant resembles that of a young porker, and squeals and grunts were of frequent occurrence as the calves kept chasing one another and frolicking among the massive pillar-like legs of their parents. In order to secure the elephants it was necessary to get the captured herd, a few at a time, into the second or securing stockade. The spectators on the platform were asked to conceal themselves. The Prince and Mr. Sanderson took up a position near the door, which had been thrown open, leading to the second enclosure. The beaters on the side furthest from the door were directed to clap their hands. Immediately the clapping began there was a stampede among the elephants. The more timid ones rushed tumultuously towards the open door ; the largest of the females turned in the direction of the beaters and, trumpeting shrilly, charged up to the stockade and kicked showers of dust and stones with her fore legs into the faces of the beaters behind the stockade. She was making some attempt to pull down the stakes in order to get at the beaters, when a shrill cry from her baby made her hurry back to the herd, now assembled near

LOWERING THE TRAP-DOOR OF THE KHEDDAH.

[*To face page* 9.

the open door. A renewed clapping of hands sent a young tusker and five large females through the entrance, when down came the ponderous door and separated them from the rest of the herd. Bang! bang! with blank cartridge into the faces of those nearest to the gate, and the herd retreated to the middle of the enclosure, where they were left for the time while the six animals on the other side were being dealt with. Among these was a very large female—with one exception the largest in the herd—which had been separated from her calf. She appeared to be nearly frantic, and made repeated charges at the door, in spite of rounds of blank cartridge fired in her face. Her charges were terrific and would probably have brought down the great door if the *koonkies*, or tame elephants, had not been sent in to secure her. Six trained female elephants, with *mahouts* (drivers) on their necks, were turned into the enclosure and endeavoured to surround the frantic mother; but she simply pushed them aside and again made for the door. Jung Bahadoor, the great fighting elephant of the Maharaja of Mysore, was then sent in, and took up a position before the gate with his formidable tusks in front, making a barrier on which the furious female would impale herself should she attempt to charge. She approached within a few yards of Jung, looked at him attentively and then trumpeted loudly, and was answered by a shrill signal from her calf on the other side. She appeared inclined even to push by the great tusker, but a warning grunt from him seemed to cow her. The *koonkies* had again approached and, close-packed behind her, had cut off her retreat. She had the tusks of Jung before her and six tame elephants jostling her behind. The famous noosers, Gunnee and Fuzlee, were soon down, and had the hobbles round her hind legs. To these a great hawser was attached, and two of the tame elephants taking the end of the hawser in their trunks commenced to drag her away from the gate. Her efforts to break from the hawser were truly marvellous. She would throw herself flat on the ground with legs spread far apart, and roll clean over on her back. Then she would rise suddenly and throw up her hind legs, exactly like a horse kicking. Again she would rise high in the air, supported on a single foot, and with trunk uplifted trumpet shrilly. I had often seen ancient Hindoo carvings representing elephants in positions that I thought to be impossible and to exist only in the designer's imagination, but after what I saw at the *kheddahs* I know that the sculptors were close observers, and that the seemingly impossible poses are really true to nature. These huge unwieldy brutes seem to have no joints, or rather one universal joint, as they can turn and twist in a manner that is truly astonishing. As all efforts to drag the recalcitrant female to a tree were unavailing she was left for the time while the other five were secured. Some were hobbled and dragged to a tree, and there made fast. Others were lassoed and secured between two tame elephants, and led out of the enclosure and fastened to posts. It was now about noon and the beaters had gone off to get

SECURING WILD ELEPHANTS WITH THE AID OF TAME ELEPHANTS.

[*To face page* 10.

their midday meal, when it was time to lift the ponderous door and let a few more elephants into the securing stockade. The few natives present were unable to lift the gate and Mr. Sanderson impressed the British officers present tc help. It was amusing to watch Captains Holford and Harvey, of the Prince's staff, Colonels Macintire and Grant, of the Maharaja's staff, Mr. Claude Vincent, of the Madras Governor's staff, Sir Oliver St. John, the British Resident, and others, take hold of the hawser supporting the door and draw it up with a "Heave, oh!" Up went the gate, and in rushed the little baby elephant, whose mother was still trying to shake off her hobbles. It was touching to watch her fondling her calf as soon as it rejoined her. She felt it all over with her trunk, thrust it from her to have a good look at it, and drew it again to her side, and repeated this a dozen times, her head wagging up and down, and her forelegs beating time as if to a dancing measure. Now and again she would put her trunk down her own throat into her stomach and draw thence a quantity of water, which she would blow over her body in a fine spray and also sprinkle over her calf. With the second batch let into the enclosure was a huge female, the largest in the herd. She was said to be very old, as the top of her ear curled forward—a sign of extreme age in elephants. This brute was very vicious, and had shown no fear of the beaters. Indeed, she had made frequent attempts to get at them by putting her trunk over the palisading. When driven into the second enclosure, and cut off from the main body of the herd, she kept running hither and thither, pulling at the log partition between the two pounds, and seemed likely to break her way through, when Sanderson ordered in six more *koonkies*—a dozen in all—to secure her.

It was thought that with a dozen trained elephants inside the enclosure there would be very little danger from the wild ones, so the Prince and Sanderson entered to get a nearer view. The *mahouts* mounted on the necks of the tame elephants are in perfect safety, as the wild ones take not the slightest notice of them, being apparently unaware that the little object on the neck of their domesticated brethren is their real source of danger. Should a rogue elephant (one that has made its escape from captivity) be among the captives, it at once attacks the *mahout*. The vicious female had been close-hemmed in by the tame elephants, and repeated unsuccessful attempts had been made to hobble or lasso her. But she was a wary brute and with her trunk threw off the lasso, and by swinging her hind legs backwards and forwards prevented the hobbles being fixed. The Prince was intently watching a young tusker being dragged to a tree, when suddenly there went up a shout, and the great female was seen to break through the encircling tame ones and rush straight in the direction of the Prince. Our hearts were in our mouths; some involuntarily closed their eyes as if to shut out the sight of an Empire's heir torn limb from limb or crushed out of human

THE DUKE OF CLARENCE CHARGED BY A WILD ELEPHANT.

[*To face page* 13.

shape. What would the scion of our Royal House do? The infuriated beast charged down on him with several tame elephants close at her heels. The Prince calmly awaited its approach, but when the brute was within a dozen paces Sanderson, who had been standing beside the Prince all the while, stepped forward, raised his hand, and shouted. Well was he called the *hathee* king! As if obedient to an order, the brute turned sharply to the left and made off. This is what actually took place, but Reuter's agent, who was not present when the incident occurred, telegraphed home the camp version of the story, and numerous were the mistaken messages sent to the Duke of Clarence from all parts of the world!

Of the thirty-seven elephants captured on this occasion, eight were shot next day by Sanderson's order, as they were too old for work and could not be tamed. I asked him why he could not let them go free rather than destroy the poor brutes. He told me that a herd consisted of a single family —youngsters, parents, grandparents, great-grandparents, sisters, cousins, aunts, *et hoc genus omne*; that the members of a herd always kept together; and that if he set some of them free they would not take themselves off, but would linger around and probably attack the camp at night. He added that, on one occasion, when he was fresh to the business of elephant-catching, he set free several old beasts, after he had removed the remainder of his captives to a camp twenty-six miles away. At night the animals he had set free stampeded his camp and nearly killed several keepers. There was no help for it, therefore, but to kill the old and useless beasts. To prevent the air being contaminated by the carcases, a large fire was kindled over their bodies and the mountain of flesh was burnt to ashes.

THE "RAJ-NAG," OR KING-COBRA.

"SAR! Sar! the village-mans bring the cock-coop" —thus shouted my boy, or Madrasee servant, as I was taking an afternoon nap in my tent of green leaves in one of the valleys of the Nullamullays, not far from the famous diamond mines of Banaganpully. I had been directed by a London syndicate to discover the mines of Buwapatam, said to be the only ones in India where diamonds are found in their true matrix. These mines were visited by Dr. Heyne as far back as 1808, but have since passed out of notice, no later writer on the diamond mines of India making any mention of them. The following is a description from "Heyne's Tracts Historical and Statistical": "I was formerly of opinion that limestone, or a compound in which lime forms the predominating constituent, would be found the matrix of the diamond. Nor was this opinion unreasonable, as in general the bed in which diamonds are found is covered or mixed with calcareous marl. But since my acquaintance with the Banaganpully mines, and with those of Buwapatam, I have been obliged to change my opinion. In the former place we find them in a conglomerate in which no calcareous admixture is discoverable, and in which an argillaceous matter—probably wacke—forms the cement; and in the latter place the mines are absolutely in mountains composed of wacke, in which I have not discovered any jasper or other pebbles. The latter mines are particularly remarkable. They are said, about eighty years ago, to have furnished the largest gems to the Nizam's collection, at all events they deserve future and particular investigation. I made an excursion to them in 1808, but when there, was so ill and so weak that I was barely able to walk to the hills where the diamond mines had been worked. They are very extensive, on a kind of table land which is intersected by ranges of hills, on which these mines wind from one to another."

I had inspected the Banaganpully mines; had then gone east to Nundial, and had been for the last week hunting up and down the gorges and hill-tops of the Nullamullays near to the famous peak of Eshwarnacoopum (God's Hill), over three thousand feet high. I had received native information which led me to believe that I would find the place of which I was in search to the north-east of the above-mentioned peak. That part of the country was said to be very heavily wooded and extremely malarious, so that none but the wild Chentsus—a race inhabiting these hills—could live there; and there were tracts so deadly that even the wild Chentsus dared not enter them. The diamond mines were said to be there, but guarded by enormous serpents of the most venomous kind. "*Raj-Nag Pamoo* (king-cobra snakes)," said my native guide. "The diamonds are the eyes of the *Raj-Nags* themselves. In those deep valleys are their burial grounds, and the largest of the serpents keep watch over the remains of their fellows. It is only by sacrificing a buffalo to *Garuda* (the eagle), the lord of the serpents, that you may obtain permission to visit them." This strange fable irresistibly recalled to my mind the story of Sinbad the Sailor and his adventure with the serpents and eagles in the valley of diamonds. Nicolo Conti, who visited this region in the early part of the fifteenth century, was apparently told the same tale, as he writes that "the mountain where the diamonds are, is infested with great and deadly serpents. The natives bring oxen, which they drive to the top of a high mountain which overtops the hill of diamonds, and here they offer sacrifice and cast the flesh of the oxen into the valley below. Diamonds sometimes adhere to the warm flesh. Great vultures and eagles, which build in the precipitous rocks, scent the flesh and swoop down into the valleys and carry the meat and adhering diamonds to their nests, and in these nests the men find diamonds enough to repay them all their labour and expense."

It was with great difficulty that I procured coolies to carry my baggage, and guides to show the way into the dense forests which clothe the low ranges of hills that lie at the foot of the eastern slope of the Nullamullays. When engaged in the forest I never carry a tent, but run up a light shelter of branches and grass, as I find this cooler and pleasanter than canvas, and it saves the carrying of tents, a most difficult job where labour is scarce and the mountain paths hard to climb.

I had engaged some Chentsus to clear a path and build the shelter of our camps, and I had quite won the heart of the headman by little presents of tobacco, so that he became very communicative, and offered to show me *shikar* (sport) of all sorts. I endeavoured to find out from him where the old diamond workings were, but he knew nothing of them, and did not even know what a diamond was when shown one. He knew of some pits on a low hill, but he said a *Raj-Nag Pamoo* had taken up its abode there, and no one would go to the place, as a *Raj-Nag* was more dreaded than a dozen man-eating tigers. I may here say that there is no denizen of the forest more dreaded than the king-cobra. Natives who would think nothing of beating up a man-eater in his favourite haunts, or bearding a bear in its cave, will shrink with dismay when asked to face this dreaded brute.

The *Ophiophagus Elaps* or King-Cobra is the fiercest and most venomous of all the serpent kind. Attaining to a length of seventeen feet—one was recently shot in the Kurnool forests which measured eighteen and a half feet—gliding over the ground at a speed which soon outstrips the swiftest man; climbing trees with ease, and more at home on the tree-tops than even the monkeys; fearlessly attacking without the slightest provocation all it meets, men or beasts, it is no wonder that the forest haunted by this terrible creature is forsaken by all other animals. Scientists tell us that the *Ophiophagus* feeds on other snakes —hence its name; but this assertion is disputed by the native *shikars* of the wild tribes found in the various forest tracts of India, who declare that the chief food of the king-cobra is young monkey, and that to secure this dainty it will lie in wait for days in the branches of the fruit-bearing trees in the forest. Birds, young pigs, deer, and wild dogs are not amiss, and it is only when other food fails that it will feed on its own kind. I have shot a king-cobra thirteen feet long, which had begun to swallow a python eight feet in length. About four feet of the body of the boa had already disappeared down the throat of the *Ophiophagus* when a charge of No. 6 shot at close range broke the latter's back. Even then it attempted to show fight, and its efforts to lift its head with four feet of flesh as thick as one's arm still hanging from its jaws, were truly marvellous.

The natives recognise three kinds of cobras, distinguished by the markings on the head. The common Cobra-di-capello, found about houses and gardens, seldom attains a greater length than six feet. It is marked with a V, or spectacle, on the hood. About the same length, but more rare, being found only in Eastern Bengal and the Sunderbunds, is the Padma-cobra or lotus-marked *Nag*. Instead of the V, it has a star or *padma* mark on the hood. The king-cobra is the rarest of all, only being found in the densest and most remote jungles. It has a black circle on the hood. It is this serpent, with its enormous hood nearly a foot in width, which, legend relates, sheltered the infant Krishna from the sun and weather. Its range is over all the wooded tracts of India. It has been shot in Travancore, on the Neilgherries, in the forests of the East Coast, in Chota Nagpore, in Assam and in Burmah. But nowhere is it found in large numbers. Although the female lays as many as eighteen eggs, most of the young are devoured by the parents, so difficult is it for these creatures to find food, as, according to the natives, nearly all small animals desert the tract in which a pair of these snakes take up their abode.

I asked Permal, the Chentsu headman, how he knew that a king-cobra had taken possession of the old pits. He said that the hill in question had been a favourite spot for snaring pea-fowl, but that about three years ago the *Raj-Nag* had come and then all other animals had left the place. He knew the *Raj-Nag* had come, because the monkeys did not answer the decoy call used by the Chentsus when trapping these creatures. This only occurred when a *Raj-Nag* was about—so their forest lore taught them. I asked him if he would lead me to the place, as I had my double-barrel gun with me, and would shoot the *Nag* if it showed itself. "The *Davaru*" (lord), he replied, "does not know the *Raj-Nag*; it is as lightning in its attack. It will be concealed in the branches or brushwood, and will dart forward and bite before you see it.

Ammavaru (the goddess *Kali*) herself cannot save you if it gets its poison fangs into you."

I told Permal I was determined to go, even if he would not go with me, as I had come to see the old pits, and the old pits I must see. After much cogitation with his fellows, he said if *Davaru* insisted on going, then he would devise a means to outdo even the *Raj-Nag*. His grandfather had done so years and years ago, when a mad gentleman who broke stones (a geologist!) had visited these parts. Permal promised to come again next day. With this the Chentsus took their departure, and we saw nothing of them till next afternoon, when my servant called out "Sar! sar! the village-mans bring the cock-coop." On going out to see what was up, I perceived Permal and another Chentsu with two enormous wicker baskets of the kind known throughout South India as cock-baskets or hen-coops. The baskets were a little larger and rather more strongly made than those ordinarily sold for penning fowls. Permal said these baskets were to be put over our heads when we got near the haunts of the king-cobra, and that we should then be perfectly safe. The meshes of the basket, he explained, were too small for the serpent's head to pass through, so that it could not bite us, and when it attacked all we had to do was to squat down with the basket over us (like a candle extinguisher) and fire at the brute through the meshes. I laughed at the idea of being cooped up in a cock-basket; but as there was no other method of inducing the Chentsus to show me the old mines, I agreed to this plan, and arranged to go next morning. Nothing would induce any of my camp-followers to accompany me, cock-coop or no cock-coop.

Starting off early next morning, we had a good ten miles to go before we got to the low hills, some two hundred feet above the broad valley of the Nullamullays, where the old pits were said to be. The jungle was very dense—giant bamboos and large forest trees, with much tall grass and undergrowth of thorns. The Chentsus stalked on in front, with the baskets on their heads. As we neared the site of the old pits, I noticed that the large trees had disappeared, but the undergrowth was more dense, showing that at one time this had been a forest clearing. Permal now advanced with great caution, and asked me to put one of the baskets over my head, he and his fellow getting under the other. After some demur I did so, and we had gone less than half-a-mile in this fashion, when suddenly a peculiar whistling noise was heard on our right. The Chentsus immediately squatted down and seized the cord hanging from the centre of the basket, so as to hold it firmly down without exposing the hands. Permal made signs to me to do the same, and said there were two king-cobras about; and that the whistle was that of the female calling to her mate, and that we should be attacked almost immediately. Down we all three squatted therefore, with the baskets over us, and firmly held on to the centre cord, so as to fix them hard on to the ground. We waited perhaps

ATTACKED BY A KING-COBRA.

five minutes in this position, but no snakes were visible. I could see the Chentsus gesticulating to one another, but could not make out what it was all about.

It was only now that I began to realise the danger of our position, and the value of the wicker baskets as a protection from a sudden attack of these fearful brutes. The undergrowth was so dense that it was impossible to see more than a yard or two around. It would not, therefore, be difficult for the snakes to attack us unperceived, nor would it be possible to use a gun before they were on us. The Chentsus still continued to gesticulate and point in my direction. Keeping a firm grasp of the rope, I turned round, and, there, above me and within eighteen inches of the top of the basket, I saw the expanded hood and gleaming eyes of the dreaded *Ophiophagus*. How it got there without my knowing it I cannot say, but there it was, looking down at me, and apparently bothered by the novel structure between it and its prey. Immediately I turned the creature set up a hissing that made my blood run cold. It resembled nothing so much as the hissing noise made by steam escaping from an engine. The hood appeared to be fully nine inches wide, and over a foot in length, and the forked tongue, which shot in and out, was quite three inches long. I began to feel quite sick and my eyes to swim, whether through the fascinating power said to be exerted by the eye of the serpent, or from the strong musky odour emitted by the snake at each hiss, or from sheer funk, I cannot say. Why I did not use my gun when I might easily have blown the head off the horrid monster, I do not know.

I now saw the utility of the cord hanging from the apex of the basket. As I felt my head spinning, I threw my weight on the cord and kept the basket firmly planted on the ground. It was well I did so, for suddenly I heard a dull thud, and then a succession of blows on the sides of the basket, and saw the great cobra wriggling on the ground endeavouring to extract with its mouth an arrow deeply imbedded in its body about three feet from the head. A second and a third arrow were now planted in its body by the Chentsus, who shot from under their basket, raising it for the purpose. I now felt a violent tug at the top of the coop, and looking up saw a second king-cobra biting the knot of the cord outside the basket, and by which I held it down, and shaking it just as a dog does a rat. The terror of that moment I cannot express. What if it should overturn the basket! The strength of thirteen feet of muscle must be enormous, and if used in the right direction would soon overcome my pull at the cord. What would then happen? Certain death for me I felt sure. Again the whiz of an arrow, and I saw a gaping wound along the neck of the fierce brute as it quitted its hold to look for this new foe. Fixing my knee on the cord, I now placed the muzzle of my gun just through one of the square openings of the basket, and, aiming at the hood, fired both barrels in rapid succession, and had the satisfaction of seeing the horrid brute fling up the leaves and dust in its death throes. I looked round for the first assailant, and found it lying in the path with several more arrows planted in it, but still biting fiercely at the arrow that had first entered its body. A shot in the head soon settled this brute also.

Permal said we might now leave the shelter of the baskets, as there could be no more full-grown king-cobras in that place. There might be very young ones, but they would not attack us. There were never more than a pair of large snakes of this species in any one locality, he added. As soon as the little ones could hunt for themselves, they went off to other places, or else fell victims to the rapacious appetites of their parents. The snakes were at once skinned by the Chentsus, who used the sharp iron heads of their arrows for this purpose. The poison fangs and glands, the palate, and the gall were carefully preserved by them for medicine. Diluted with gingelly oil, the poison is drunk in small portions, and is said to be a wonderful preservative against all snake-bites.

I measured the skins when we got home late that evening. The larger one was fourteen feet eight inches, and the other thirteen feet. Leaving the younger of the Chentsus to finish the skinning, I went on with Permal to visit the old diamond mines, and there a most singular adventure befell me; but I must reserve this for another chapter.

ALADDIN'S CAVE.

In my account of the destruction of the king-cobras, I promised to relate a very strange adventure that befell me at the old diamond mines of Buwapatam.

Permal led the way to the old pits, which were situated on some rising ground a little way to the east. He said there were several hundreds of these pits extending over some miles of ground, but that they were more numerous and larger just at the spot we were now visiting. Mounds of earth, probably excavated from the digging, marked the mouth of each pit. A dense, thorny vegetation grew around and overhung the entrance of the shafts and concealed it from view, so that one might easily stumble into one of these traps, or pitfalls, which, indeed, they closely resembled. Selecting one of the largest and best preserved of the pits for examination, the Chentsu's axe quickly cleared away the brushwood. A strong, light rope, which I always carry on these expeditions, was fastened to a stump, and I prepared to descend the old mine, but, before doing so, I threw in a wisp of lighted grass to test the condition of the air—a very needful precaution—and to get some idea of the depth I would have to descend. The grass kept alight at the bottom of the pit, showing the air was fit to breathe, and the depth appearing to be not more than thirty feet, I began the descent, first sticking a lighted candle to a piece of damp clay attached—miner fashion —to my cap. On arriving at the bottom, I found myself on the top of a mound of *debris* fallen in from the mouth of the pit. The ground sloped away on all sides, to a very considerable distance, making a very large chamber, the full extent of which I could not see, owing to the darkness, the glimmering light of my candle not extending very far. After waiting a little time, to accustom my eyes to the darkness, I proceeded to examine the sides, in order to discover the nature of the "working," and whether it was for diamonds or some other mineral. On approaching the side, I suddenly found it sparkling with gleams of gold and green and red light, as if studded all over with gems, from which the light I held in my hand was scintillated and refracted. Turning round, I found a similar twinkling light all round on the walls of the mine, as if ten thousand fire-flies had settled all over the sides, only that the light differed in colour, there being sparkles of white and red and green. Was this a veritable Aladdin's Cave, and were all these glints of light flashing from real diamonds, rubies, and emeralds!

The adventure of the early part of the day had given me cause to believe that there was at least some foundation of truth in the stories of the

"Thousand and One Nights." Could this be the same cave in which Aladdin was shut up by the cruel magician? And were all those diamonds and rubies and emeralds, within my reach? It only wanted a Genius of the Ring to complete the illusion. Great Heavens! What was that? A distinct hiss as of a cat, and then in the distance a gigantic cat itself. As I looked it appeared to grow in size and swell to enormous dimensions. A veritable Genius, and this the enchanted cave! With my heart in my mouth, I hurried back to the mound in the centre of the shaft, and shouted to Permal to join me and bring my gun with him. I had now time to collect my thoughts and try to work out some explanation of this strange adventure. Experience had long ago taught me that diamonds, rubies, and emeralds are never found together in their natural state, and I was also aware that these gems do not reflect light or sparkle to any extent in their uncut condition. Perhaps it might be a mica mine, and the light be reflected from flakes of that mineral. But what about the monstrous cat? Was that the result of imagination, or stern reality? There was no mistaking the hiss and growl, which again emanated from a far corner of the mine on our throwing a stone in that direction. Permal at once declared that he could smell tiger. He kept sniffing about, and said, "*Ullee, davaru* (tiger, my lord)." The strange sparkles of light still kept twinkling around, as if innumerable stars were set in the walls. I noticed, however, that, if we attempted to move, thus agitating the air, the scintillation would be more brilliant. Cutting up several candles into pieces, we soon had a brilliant light about us, and this enabled me to see that the underground chamber was very irregular in shape, about thirty feet wide from east to west, and somewhat longer towards the north. It was from the latter direction that the hissing and growling seemed to come, and Permal declared he could see a large tiger crouching down behind a piece of rock in the far corner. But if it was a tiger, why did not it attack us, as it could not be more than twenty paces away from us ? I was inclined to believe it was a hyena, and therefore plucked up heart to have a shot at it, as I would not have ventured to attack a tiger at such close quarters, and on foot. Cocking both barrels, I directed Permal to throw stones at the creature to induce it to break cover ; but no, the brute would not move, but continued spitting and growling. I was now convinced it was a hyena, and advanced more boldly until I could just see a dark object behind a rock. I could see the gleaming eyes distinctly, so, taking careful aim, I fired, and then retreated hastily to the mound. We waited some time, but could hear no sound, and the smoke made it more difficult to see. We threw several large stones in the direction, but there was no movement. The hissing, too, had ceased. Re-loading the empty barrel, we again advanced cautiously, and then I made out the body, in the same position apparently. Again aiming carefully, I tried a second shot. There was no missing so large an object within a few paces, so I felt quite sure the creature was hit, but not so sure that it was dead. We retreated once more to the mound, and after some time advanced again to the attack, but not a movement had taken place in the object. Feeling quite sure it was dead, we now got close up and examined it, and found it to be a tiger of the largest size, in a most emaciated condition—nothing but skin and bone. Probably its last effort was to rise on its legs on my first intrusion. It had not strength for any further effort and must have died in a day or two from sheer starvation. The Chentsu surmised that it had fallen into this natural trap while in pursuit of wild pig, and I could well understand the tiger's inability to get out again, as the widening out of the chamber began about fifteen feet above our heads, so that it would require a leap of that height in order to fasten its claws into the narrow neck of the shaft, which was shaped somewhat like a Florentine flask.

Emaciated as it was, there was no use attempting to draw that weight of skin and bone up the shaft. It was as much as our united efforts could do to drag it to the mound. Here Permal proceeded to flay it, while I continued my examination of the cave. The sides were covered with a dense growth of moss, with here and there a fern and lichen. This growth seemed to confine itself to a bed of conglomerate about three feet thick. I had no difficulty in recognising this as one of the beds of the Kurnool series, known to be diamondiferous in many parts of South India. I knew it was hopeless looking for diamonds *in situ*, but I took samples of the conglomerate for further testing. There was nothing to show whence the strange gleams of light had come—not a trace of mica was to be seen anywhere. The sparkling had now entirely disappeared, and to this day I have been unable to account for it, nor could the friends I consulted give any explanation of it. Permal also had seen the lights, so it was not due to my imagination.

After the tiger was flayed we tied the skin to the rope. I then made my way up, hand over hand, and the Chentsu followed, and together we drew up the skin. On examination it proved to be in splendid condition, the fur being beautifully soft and long. It measured ten feet one inch from snout to tip of tail, and from ridge of shoulder to fore-claws three feet ten inches; so that it must have stood a greater height than most tigers. Thus, two king-cobras and a large tiger were the spoils of one of the most exciting day's adventures I have ever experienced in all my journeyings in the wild places of India.

MY SHIKAREE FRIENDS.

I.—PANDU THE GOND.

How little do we know of India even after a hundred and fifty years' occupation of the country! Off the beaten tracks—the great trunk roads, the well-known lines of railway—and we are lost in a wilderness of peoples and things of whose existence we know nothing unless we search the pages of the Gazetteer, and even that often fails us, since however carefully compiled, its information is chiefly derived from European sources—and Europeans as a rule are slow to win the confidence of the natives. I do not claim to be anything very different from my fellows, but perhaps from constant association with wild tribes in various parts of India, I have learned to appreciate their many virtues. I have found them as staunch and as true as men of my own blood, and have come to look on their little failings with a kindly eye. However, I am not writing a dissertation on ethnology; I merely wish to describe some of my *shikaree* friends.

Let me begin, then, with a pen-and-ink sketch of Pandu, the hunter. Tall for a native, nearly six feet high, and a frame so gaunt that he would not take a bad place in a skeleton show, yet withal as straight as a reed and with an eye as keen as a hawk's. Not the slightest thing moves in the forest but his keen vision or sharp ears detect it. He must be over fifty, as his scanty locks and long moustache are quite grey; yet he thinks nothing of a forty-mile trudge beside my pony, and is up and away for *khubber* (early news) as soon as we get into camp, as if the long walk were nothing more than his regular morning exercise. I have known him go twenty-four hours without food or drink, beyond a pinch of snuff thrown into his mouth wherever I have stopped for a rest. By caste a Gond, he will not touch cooked food from my hands, but will gratefully accept a handful of rice, which he eats raw by preference. Armed with an old Brown Bess (army musket), presented to him years ago by Mr. Hewett, a former Commissioner of Chota Nagpore, he is an unerring shot, and will fearlessly face a wounded tiger or raging buffalo. He makes his own powder, purchasing the sulphur and saltpetre at Ranchi and burning some twigs of the Hilla bush for his charcoal. He also fashions his own bullets, in rude moulds of clay. But his great difficulty is the percussion caps. These are extremely difficult to be got, now that breech-loading small arms are in general use; and I won his heart by a present of several hundred of the large caps of the kind used with the old Brown Bess. He has frequently asked me if I could not convert his cap-gun into a flint-lock, as with the latter there would be no bother about caps. Clothing does not trouble Pandu. A narrow cotton cloth wrapped round the loins is his only garment. A bag, somewhat like a soldier's haversack, is suspended from his shoulder, and in this are carried all his belongings when on the march. Powder-horn, lead pellets, a rag containing the caps, an old clasp-knife, a little opium, a little tobacco, and a *seer* or two of rice, and Pandu is ready for a journey of a week's duration. He has enormous hands and feet—I don't know that I have ever seen a human being with larger. The fingers are very long, the thumb being short. The sharpest rocks seem to have no effect on the horny soles of his feet, and he uses no covering for his head even in the hottest day in May.

Pandu first attached himself to my camp in the Chota Nagpore district several years ago. Scarcely a day passed but he brought me in a pea-fowl, green pigeon, jungle cock, or teal, and occasionally a haunch of venison. Pandu dearly loved venison days, because then he was certain of *buksheesh* (a present), and this he spent in a regular carouse on rice-beer. Rice-beer can only be had at Somij on Sundays, as on that day the coolies get their weekly wage and a *hât*, or bazaar, is held under the mango tree near the village. I soon noticed that it was on Sundays also that Pandu brought his venison, and on questioning him he smiled and said: "The Sahib's luck is great, even the deer cannot withstand it." The amount of rice-beer that Pandu could drink was simply astonishing. I am afraid to say how much, but it was certainly not less than three gallons. Leaf-cup after leaf-cup would be drained, and beyond a grunt of satisfaction and an endearing word to Motee, his little *shikaree* bullock and constant companion, he would continue drinking till he spent all his money at one sitting. A favourite expression of his to denote his poverty was, that " the skin of his stomach adhered to his backbone." This was almost literally true, for he was painfully emaciated. On an occasion like this however his abdomen would visibly swell, till he resembled a water-bag mounted on two sticks. When he had drunk his " skinful " Pandu would stand with his back leaning against a tree, one foot resting on the other, his head bent forward and his hands hanging straight down. He would stand in this position for hours, muttering to himself, the vigilant Motee keeping watch the while and allowing no one, man or beast, to approach his master.

I have read of the affection of a dog for its master, but nothing could surpass the devotion of this little bullock to Pandu. Motee (the pearl) was an ordinary Indian bullock, about four feet high and of the whitey-brown colour common among the stunted cattle in native villages. He was thoroughly trained to *shikar* by Pandu, and seemed to comprehend his master's wishes intuitively. A glance, and Motee would move forward or backward, as required. A motion of the finger, and he would lie down or kick up his heels and rush about as if mad. Pandu did all his stalking with the aid of this bullock, and much of his success depended on its intelligence.

An old piece of sacking, painted with green daubs on one side to resemble shrubbery, on the other side with bars of vivid red, was thrown over Motee's back like a horse-cloth, and hanging down to the ground effectually concealed the crouching hunter. Did he wish to stalk antelope, then the red bars were exposed, and Motee would graze quietly in a direction oblique yet approaching the herd. The bright bars would attract the curiosity of the deer, and they would approach so near as to allow of an unfailing shot from Pandu's place of concealment under the stomach of the bullock. Was it a flock of pea-fowl that was in sight, then the green side of the sacking would be turned towards the birds, and the same stealthy approach made, the pea-fowl exhibiting no alarm, as the village cattle commonly range the forests in their neighbourhood. Motee evidently took a delight in *shikar*, as he was on the alert and frisked about immediately the old man shouldered his gun. When the game was killed—and Pandu seldom missed—the little bullock would come up for his caress. If he missed, Motee would smell the gun, as if he thought there was something wrong there.

On one occasion I had the bad taste to offer the old man fifty rupees for his bullock. I was heartily ashamed of myself immediately afterwards, for the look of distress on Pandu's face I shall never forget. "Sahib," said the old man, with tears in his eyes, "if you knew all that Motee is to me, if you knew that he has repeatedly saved my life, you would not make me such an offer. What is money to me?

I would only drink it in a little time, and then what would I do? Motee is my life; he cheers me, he helps me, he looks after me. I once had a wife and son; both are gone; but I have Motee, and I live. If Motee dies, I will die too!" Poor old man! I really believe he would die if anything happened to Motee. Old, drunken, degraded, and stupid as he is, I have still an affectionate regard for Pandu, and number him among my *shikaree* friends.

"PEER BUX," THE TERROR OF HUNSUR.

PEER BUX was the largest elephant in the Madras Government Commissariat Department. He stood nine feet six inches at the shoulder and more than ten feet at the highest point of the convexity of the backbone. His tusks protruded three and a half feet and were massive and solid, with a slight curve upwards and outwards. His trunk was large and massive, while the skin was soft as velvet and mottled red and white, as high-class elephants' should be. His pillar-like fore legs were as straight as a bee line from shoulder to foot, and showed muscle enough for half-a-dozen elephants. Physically Peer Bux was the beau ideal of elephantine beauty, a brute that should have fetched fifteen thousand rupees in the market and be cheap at that price, for was he not a grander elephant to look at than many a beast that had cost its princely owner double that sum? He was quiet too and docile, and could generally be driven by a child. Yet with all his good qualities, with all his majestic proportions, Peer Bux was tabooed by the natives. No Hindoo would have him at a gift. He was a marked beast; *his tail was bifurcated at the extremity.* This signified, said those natives learned in elephant lore, that he would one day take human life.

When captured in the *kheddahs* in Michael's Valley, Coimbatore district, the European official in charge of the *kheddah* operations imagined the animal would bring a fancy price; but at the public sale of the captured herd no one would give a bid for him, although his tusks alone would have fetched over a thousand rupees for their ivory. The fatal blemish—the divided tail—was soon known to intending purchasers, and there being no bidders he had to be retained for Government use.

The Commissariat Department was justly proud of Peer Bux. He had done good service for six years. Did the heavy guns stick in the mud when the artillery was on its way to Bellary, Peer Bux was sent to assist, and with a push of his massive head he would lift the great cannon, however deep its wheels might be imbedded in the unctuous black cotton soil. Were heavy stores required at Mercara, Peer Bux would mount the steep ghaut road, and think nothing of a ton and a half load on his back. The Forest Department too found him invaluable in drawing heavy logs from the heart of the reserves. His register of conduct was blameless, and beyond occasional fits of temper during the *must* season once a year he was one of the most even-tempered as well as one of the most useful beasts in the Transport establishment.

The Commissariat sergeant at Hunsur, who had

known Peer Bux for two years, would smile when allusion was made to his bifurcated tail and the native superstition regarding that malformation. "Look up his register," he would say; "no man-killing there. Why I would rather trust him than any other elephant, male or female, in the lines. Just you see that little beggar, no higher than this" (showing his walking cane), "the *mahout's* son, take him out to the jungles and bring him back loaded with fodder, and lambaste him too, if he won't obey the little imp. He kill a man! Why he wouldn't kill a fly. The niggers know nothing; they are a superstitious lot."

But a little while, and quite another story had to be told of Peer Bux. This pattern animal had gone *must*. Fazul, his usual *mahout* (keeper), was not there to manage him (he had gone with Sanderson to Assam), and the new keeper had struck Peer Bux when he showed temper, and had been torn limb from limb by the irritated brute. Peer Bux had broken his chains; had stampeded the Amrut-mahal cattle at Hunsur; had broken into the Government harness and boot factory and done incredible damage; had gone off on the rampage, on the Manantoddy road; had overturned coffee carts and scattered their contents on the road; had killed several cart-men; had looted several villages and torn down the huts. In fact a homicidal mania seemed to have come over him, as he would steal into the *cholum* (sorghum millet) fields and pull down the *machans* (bamboo platforms) on which the cultivator sat watching his corn by night, and tear the poor wretch to pieces or trample him out of all shape, and it was even said that in his blind rage he would eat portions of his human victims. I may here mention that natives firmly believe that elephants will occasionally take to man-eating. It is a common practice when a tiger is killed for the *mahouts* to dip balls of *jaggery* (coarse sugar) in the tiger's blood and feed the elephants that took part in the drive with this mess. They say the taste of the tiger's blood gives the elephant courage to face these fierce brutes. The taste for blood thus acquired sticks to the elephant, and when he goes mad or *must* and takes to killing human beings, some of their blood gets into his mouth and reminds him of the sugar and blood given him at the tiger-hunts, and he occasionally indulges in a mouthful of raw flesh.

Was Peer Bux *must*, or was he really mad? The *mahouts* at Hunsur, who knew him well, said he was only *must*. Europeans frequently speak of *must* elephants as "mad" elephants, as though the two terms were synonymous. *Must*, I may state, is a periodical functional derangement common to all bull elephants, and corresponds to the rutting season with deer and other animals. It generally occurs in the male once a year (usually in March or April), and lasts about two or three months. During this period a dark-coloured mucous discharge oozes from the temples. If this discharge is carefully washed off twice a day, and the elephant given a certain amount of opium with his food and made to stand up to his middle in water for an hour every day, beyond a little uneasiness and irritability in temper no evil consequences ensue; but should these precautions be neglected, the animal becomes savage and even furious for a time, so that it is never safe to approach him during these periods. When an elephant shows signs of *must*—the dark discharge at the temples is an infallible sign—he should always be securely hobbled and chained. A *must* elephant, even when he breaks loose and does a lot of damage, can if recaptured be broken to discipline and will become as docile as ever, after the *must* period is passed.

It is wholly different with a mad elephant. These brutes should be destroyed at once, as they never recover their senses, the derangement in their case being cerebral and permanent, and not merely functional. This madness is frequently due to sunstroke, as elephants are by nature fitted to live under the deep shade of primeval forests. In the wild state they feed only at night, when they come out into the open. They retire at dawn into the depths of the forests, so that they are never exposed to the full heat of the noonday sun.

Peer Bux being the property of the Madras Government, permission was asked to destroy him, as he had done much damage to life and property in that portion of the Mysore territory lying between Hunsur and the frontier of Coorg and North Wynaad. The Commissariat

Department however regarded him as too valuable an animal to be shot, and advised that some attempt should be made to recapture him with the aid of tame elephants. Several trained elephants were sent up from Coimbatore, some more were obtained from the Mysore State, and several hunts were organised; but all attempts at his recapture entirely failed. The great length of his fore-legs gave Peer Bux an enormous stretch, so that he could easily outpace the fleetest *shikar* elephants; and when he showed fight, none of the tuskers, not even the famous Jung Bahadoor, the fighting elephant of the Maharaja of Mysore, could withstand his charge. Meanwhile so great was the terror he inspired that nearly all traffic was stopped between Hunsur and Coorg, and Mysore and Manantoddy. He had been at large now for nearly two months, and in that time was known to have killed fourteen persons, wrecked two villages, and done an incredible amount of damage to traffic and crops. In an evil moment for himself he took it into his head to stampede the Collector's camp on the Wynaad frontier. The Collector was away at Manantoddy, but his tents and belongings were destroyed, and one camp follower killed. Permission was now obtained to destroy him by any means, and a Government reward was offered to any one who would kill the brute.

Several parties went out from Bangalore in the hope of bagging him, but never got sight of him. He was here to-day, and twenty miles off next day. He was never known to attack Europeans. He would lie in wait in some unfrequented part of the road and allow any suspicious-looking object to pass; but when he saw a line of native carts, or a small company of native travellers, he would rush out with a scream and a trumpet and overturn carts and kick them to pieces, and woe betide the unfortunate human being that fell into his clutches! He would smash them to a pulp beneath his huge feet, or tear them limb from limb.

Much of the above information regarding Peer Bux was gleaned at the Dâk Bungalow (travellers' rest-house) at Hunsur, where a party of four, including myself, were staying while engaged in a shooting trip along that belt of forest which forms the boundary between Mysore and British territory to the south-west. Our shoot thus far had been very unsuccessful. Beyond a few spotted deer and some game birds we had bagged nothing. The Government notification of a reward for the destruction of the rogue-elephant stared us in the face at every turn we took in the long, cool verandah of the bungalow. We had not come out prepared for elephant-shooting, yet there was a sufficiency of heavy metal in our armoury, we thought, to try conclusions with even so formidable an antagonist as Peer Bux, should we meet with him. Disgust at the want of success hitherto of our *shikar* expedition, and the tantalizing effects of the Government notice showing that there was game very much in evidence if we cared to go after it, soon determined our movements. The native *shikaris* were summoned, and after much consultation we shifted camp to Karkankotee, a smaller village in the State forest of that name, and on the high road to Manantoddy. The travellers' bungalow there, a second-class one, was deserted by its usual native attendants, as the rogue-elephant had paid two visits to that place and had pulled down a portion of the out-offices in his attempts to get at the servants. In the village we found only a family of Kurambas left in charge by the *Potail* (village magistrate) when the inhabitants deserted it. These people, we found, had erected for themselves a *machan* (platform) on the trees, to which they retired at night to be out of the reach of the elephant, should he come that way. From them we learned that the rogue had not been seen for a week, but that it was about his time to come that way, as he had a practice of making a complete circuit of the country lying between the frontier and the Manantoddy-Mysore and Hunsur-Mercara roads. This was good news, so we set to work at once, getting ammunition ready for this the largest of all game. Nothing less than eight drams of powder and a hardened solid ball would content most of us. K——, poor fellow, had been reading up "Smooth-bore" or some other authority on Indian game, and pinned his faith to a twelve-bore duck gun, "for," he argued, "at twenty paces"—and that was the maximum distance from which to shoot at an elephant—"the smooth-bore will shoot as straight as the rifle and hit quite as hard."

Our horses and pack-bullocks were picketed within one of the out-offices, and all the native servants took shelter inside the other. Great fires were kindled before the out-offices as a precautionary measure—not that we expected the elephant that night. We were in bed betimes, as we meant to be up at daybreak and have a good hunt all round, under the guidance of the Kurambas, who promised to take us to the rogue's favourite haunts when in that neighbourhood. The dâk-bungalow had but two rooms. That in which O—— and myself slept had a window overlooking the out-offices. In the adjacent room slept F—— and K——. Towards the small hours of the morning I was awakened by a loud discharge of fire-arms from F——'s room, followed by the unmistakable fierce trumpeting of an enraged elephant. There is no mistaking that sound when once heard. Catching up our rifles we rushed into the next room and found F——, gun in hand, peering out through the broken window frame, and K—— trying to strike a light. When F—— had recovered sufficiently from his excitement, he explained that he had been awakened by something trying to encircle his feet through the thick folds of the rug he had wrapped round them. On looking up he thought he could make out the trunk of an elephant thrust through the opening where a pane of glass had been broken in the window. His loaded gun was in the corner by his side, and, aiming at what he thought would be the direction of the head, he fired both barrels at once. With a loud scream the elephant withdrew its trunk, smashing the whole window at the same time. He had reloaded and was looking out for the elephant, in case it should return to the attack, but could see nothing, as it was too dark. F——'s was a narrow escape, for had the elephant succeeded in getting his trunk round one of his legs nothing could have saved him. With one jerk he would have been pulled through the window and quickly done to death beneath the huge feet of the brute. The thick folds of the blanket alone saved him, and even that would have been pulled aside in a little time if he had not awakened and had the presence of mind to fire at the beast.

No amount of shouting would bring any of the servants from their retreat in the out-office, although we could distinctly hear them talking to each other in low tones; and it was scarcely fair of us to ask them to come out, with the probability of an infuriated rogue elephant being about. However, we soon remembered this fact, and helping ourselves to whisky pegs, as the excitement had made us thirsty, we determined to sit out the darkness, as nothing could be done till morning.

At the first break of day, we sallied out to learn the effects of F——'s shots. We could distinctly trace the huge impressions of the elephant's feet to the forest skirting the bungalow, but could find no trace of blood. The Kuramba trackers were soon on the spot, and on matters being explained to them they said the elephant must be badly wounded about the face, otherwise he would have renewed the attack. The shots being fired at such close quarters must have scorched the opening of the wound and prevented the immediate flow of blood. They added that if wounded the elephant would not go far, but would make for the nearest water in search of mud with which to plaster the wound, as mud was a sovereign remedy for all elephant wounds, and all elephants used it. The brute would then lie up in some dense thicket for a day or two, as any exertion would tend to re-open the wound. The Kurambas appeared to be so thoroughly acquainted with the habits of these beasts, that we readily placed ourselves under their guidance, and swallowing a hasty breakfast we set off on the trail, taking with us one *shikar* to interpret and a gun-bearer, named Suliman, to carry a tiffin-basket.

The tracks ran parallel with the road for about a mile, and then crossed it and made south in the direction of the Kabbany river, an affluent of the Cauvery. Distinct traces of blood could now be seen, and presently we came to a spot covered with blood, where the elephant had evidently stood for some time. The country became more and more difficult as we approached the river. Dense clumps of bamboo and wait-a-bit thorns, with here and there a large teak or honne tree, made it difficult to see more than a few yards ahead. The Kuramba guides said that we must now advance more cautiously, as the river was within half a mile, and that we might come on the "rogue" at any moment. Up to this moment, I don't know if any of us appreciated the full extent of the danger we were running. Following up a wounded *must* elephant on foot, in dense cover such as we were in, meant that if we did not drop the brute with the first shot, one or more of us would in all probability pay for our temerity with our lives. We had been on the tramp two hours and we were all of us more or less excited, so taking a sip of cold tea to steady our nerves, we settled on a plan of operations. F—— and I, having the heaviest guns, were to lead, the Kuramba trackers being a pace or two in advance of us. O—— and K—— were to follow about five paces behind, and the *shikari* and Suliman were to bring up the rear at an interval of ten paces. If we came on the elephant, the advance party were to fire first and then move aside. If the brute survived our fire, the second battery would surely account for it. It never entered our minds that anything living could withstand a discharge at close quarters of eight such barrels as we carried. Having settled matters to our satisfaction, off we set on the trail, moving now very cautiously, the guides enjoining the strictest silence. Every bush was carefully examined, every thicket scanned before an advance was made; frequent stops were made, and the drops of blood carefully examined to see if they were clotted or not, as by this the Kurambas could tell how far off the wounded brute was. The excitement was intense. The rustle of a falling leaf would set our hearts pit-a-pat. The nervous strain was too great, and I began to feel quite sick. The trail now entered a cart-track through the forest, so that we could see twenty paces or so ahead. Now we were approaching the river, for we could hear the murmuring of the water some two or three hundred yards ahead. The bamboo clumps grew thicker on either side. The leading Kuramba was just indicating that the trail led off to the right, when a terrific trumpet directly behind us made us start round, and a ghastly sight met our view. The elephant had evidently scented us long before we appeared in view, and had left the cart-track and, making a slight *détour* to the right, had gone back a little way and concealed itself behind some bamboo clumps near the track. It had quietly allowed us to pass, and then, uttering a shrill scream, charged on the rear. Seizing Suliman in its trunk, it had lifted him aloft prior to dashing him to the ground, when we turned. K—— was standing in the path, about ten paces from the elephant, with his gun levelled at the brute. "Fire, K——, fire!" we shouted, but it was too late. Down came the trunk, and the body of poor Suliman, hurled with terrific force, was dashed on the ground with a sickening thud, which told us he was beyond help. As the trunk was coming down K—— fired. In a moment the enraged brute was on him. We heard a second shot, and then saw poor K—— and his gun flying through the air from a kick from the animal's fore-foot. There was no time to aim. Indeed, there was nothing to aim at, as all we could see was a great black object coming down on us with incredible speed. Four shots in rapid succession, and the brute swerved to the left and went off screaming and crashing through the bamboos in its wild flight. Rapidly reloading we waited to see if the rogue would come back, but we heard the crashing of the underwood further off and knew it had gone for good. We had now time to look round. The body of K—— we found on the top of a bamboo clump a good many yards away. We thought he was dead, as he did not reply to our calls, but on cutting down the bamboos and removing the body we found he had only swooned. A glass of whisky soon brought him round, but he was unable to move, as his spine was injured and several ribs broken. Rigging a hammock, we had him carried into Manantoddy, where he was on the doctor's hands for months before he was able to move, and finally he had to go back to England and, I believe, never thoroughly recovered his health. Suliman's corpse had to be taken into Antarasante, and after an inquest by the native Magistrate it was made over to the poor fellow's co-religionists for burial.

The subsequent history of Peer Bux—how he killed two English officers and afterwards met his own fate—I must reserve for another chapter.

THE TERROR OF HUNSUR.—II.

OUR tragic adventure with Peer Bux, the rogue elephant, related in the last chapter, was soon noised abroad and served only to attract a greater number of British sportsmen, bent on trying conclusions with the "Terror of Hunsur," as this notorious brute came to be called by the inhabitants of the adjacent districts. A month had elapsed since our ill-fated expedition, and nothing had been heard of the rogue, although its known haunts had been scoured by some of the most noted *shikars* of South India. We began to think that the wounds it had received in its encounter with us had proved fatal, and even contemplated claiming its tusks should its carcase be found, and presenting them to K—— as a memento of his terrible experience with the monster, but it was a case of "counting your chickens," for evidence was soon forthcoming that its tusks were not to be had for the asking. The beast had evidently been lying low while its wounds healed, and had retreated for this purpose into some of the dense fastnesses of the Begur jungles. Among others who arrived on the scene at this time to do battle with the Terror were two young officers from Cannanore—one a subaltern in a native regiment, the other a naval officer on a visit to that station. They had come with letters of introduction to Colonel M—— in charge of the Amrat Mahal at Hunsur, and that officer had done all in his power to dissuade the youngsters from going after the "rogue," as he saw plainly that they were green at *shikar* and did not fully comprehend the risks they would be running, nor had they experience enough to enable them to provide against possible contingencies. Finding however that dissuasion only strengthened their determination to brave all danger, he thought he would do the next best thing by giving them the best mount possible for such a task. Among the recent arrivals at the Commissariat lines was "Dod Kempa" (the Great Red One), a famous tusker sent down all the way from Secunderabad to do battle with Peer Bux. Dod Kempa was known to be staunch, as he had been frequently used for tiger-shooting in the notorious Nirmul jungles and had unflinchingly stood the charge of a wounded tiger. His *mahout* declared that the Terror of Hunsur would run at the mere sight of Dod Kempa, for had not his reputation gone forth throughout the length and breadth of India, even among the elephant folk? Kempa was not as tall as Peer Bux, but was more sturdily built, with short, massive tusks. He was mottled all over his body with red spots: hence his name Kempa (red). He was a veritable bull-dog among elephants and was by no means a handsome brute, but he had repeatedly done good service in bringing to order recalcitrant pachyderms, and for this reason had been singled out to try conclusions with the Hunsur rogue. With such a mount Colonel M—— thought the young fellows would be safe even should they meet the "Terror," so seeing them safely mounted on the pad he bid them not to fail to call on D——, the Forest officer on the Coorg frontier, who would put them up to the best means of finding the game they were after.

They had been gone about four days when one morning the Commissariat sergeant turned up at Colonel M——'s bungalow and with a salute informed him that Dod Kempa was in the lines, and that his *mahout* was drunk and incapable and he could get no information from him. The elephant and *mahout* had turned up some time during the night; the pad had been left behind, and the man could give no information about the two sahibs who had gone out with him. Fearing the worst, the Colonel sent for the *mahout*, but before the order could be carried out, a crowd of *mahouts* (elephant drivers) and other natives were seen approaching, shouting "*Pawgalee hogiya! Pawgalee hogiya!* (he has gone mad! he has gone mad!)." Yes, sure enough, there was Dod Kempa's *mahout* inanely grinning and shaking his hands. Now and again he would stop and look behind, and a look of terror would come into his eyes. He would crouch down and put his hands to his ears as if to shut out some dreadful sound. He would remain like this for a minute or two, glance furtively around, and then as if reassured would get up and smile and shake his hands. It was plainly not liquor that made him behave in this manner ; the poor fellow had actually become an imbecile through fear. It was hopeless attempting to get any information from such an object, so handing him over to the care of the medical officer, a search party mounted on elephants was at once organised and sent off in the direction of Frazerpett, twenty-four miles distant, where D——'s camp was. When they got about half-way they were met by a native forest ranger, who asked them to stop and come back with him to a country cart that followed, in which were the dead bodies of the two unfortunate officers of whom they were in search. On coming up with the cart and examining its contents a most gruesome sight met their eyes. There, rolled up in a native *kumbly* (blanket), was an indistinguishable mass of human flesh, mud, and clothing. Crushed out of all shape, the bodies were inextricably mixed together, puddled into one mass by the great feet of the *must* elephant. None dared touch the shapeless heap, where nought but the boot-covered feet were distinguishable to show that two human beings lay there. A deep gloom fell on all, natives and Europeans alike ; none dared speak above a whisper, and in silence the search party turned back, taking with them what was once two gallant young officers, but now an object that made anyone shudder to look at. The forest ranger's story was soon told : he had been an eye-witness of the tragic occurrence. Here it is :—

"The officers arrived two days ago at Periyapatna, a large village half-way to Frazerpett, and while camped there, a native brought in information of a bullock having been killed at his village some four miles off. The *Sahibs* determined to sit up in a *machan* over the kill, and do for the tiger when he returned to his meal. They left their camp-followers and baggage at Periyapatna, and accompanied only by himself (the ranger) and the native who brought the information, they rode out on Dod Kempa, took their places on the *machan*, and sent the mahout back with the elephant with orders for him to come back at dawn next day to take them back to camp. The tiger did not turn up that night, and the whole party were on their way back to Periyapatna in the early dawn, when suddenly Dod Kempa stopped, and striking the ground with the end of his trunk, made that peculiar drumming noise which is the usual signal of alarm with these animals when they scent tiger or other danger. It was still early morning, so that they could barely see any object in the shadow of the forest trees. The elephant now began to back, curl away his trunk, and sway his head from side to side. The *mahout* said he was about to charge, and that there must be another elephant in the path. We could barely keep our seats on the pad, so violent was the motion caused by the elephant backing and swaying from side to side. The officers had to hold on tight by the ropes, so that they could not use their guns, when there in the distance, only fifty yards off, we saw an enormous elephant coming towards us! There was no doubt that it was the rogue, from its great size. It had not seen us yet, as elephants see very badly; but Dod Kempa had scented him out as the wind was in our favour. The *Sahibs* urged the *mahout* to keep his elephant quiet so that they might use their guns, but it was no use, for although he cruelly beat the beast about the head with his iron goad yet it continued to back and sway. The rogue had now got within thirty yards, when it perceived us and stopped. It backed a few paces and with ears thrown forward uttered trumpet after trumpet and then came full charge down on us. No sooner did Dod Kempa hear the trumpeting than he turned round and bolted off into the forest, crashing through the brushwood and under the branches of the large trees, the *must* elephant in hot pursuit. Suddenly an overhanging branch caught in the side of the pad, ripped it clean off the elephant's back, and threw the two officers on the ground. I managed to seize the branch and clambered up out of harm's way. When I recovered a little from my fright, I saw the rogue elephant crushing something up under its fore feet. Now and again it would stoop and drive its tusks into the mass and begin stamping on it again. This it did for about a quarter of an hour. It then went off in the direction that Dod Kempa had taken. I saw nothing of Dod Kempa after the pad fell off. I waited for two hours, and seeing the mad elephant did not come back, I got down and ran to Periyapatna and told the *Sahibs'* servants, and we went back with a lot of people, and found that the mass the elephant had been crushing under its feet was the bodies of the two officers! The brute must have caught them when they were thrown to the ground and killed them with a blow of its trunk or a crush of the foot, and it had then mangled the two bodies together. We got a cart and brought the bodies away."

Simple in all its ghastly details, the tale was enough to make one's blood run cold, but heard as it was, said one present, "within a few yards of what that bundle of native blankets contained, it steeled one's heart for revenge." But let us leave this painful narrative and hasten on to the time when the monster met with his deserts at the hand of one of the finest sportsmen that ever lived, and that too in a manner which makes every Britisher feel a pride in his race that can produce such men.

Gordon Cumming was a noted *shikari*, almost as famous in his way as his brother, the celebrated lion-slayer of South Africa, and his equally famous sister, the talented artist and explorer of Maori fastnesses in New Zealand. Standing over six feet in his stockings and of proportionate breadth of shoulder, he was an athlete in every sense of the word. With his heavy double rifle over his shoulder, and with Yalloo, his native tracker and *shikari* at his heels, he would think nothing of a twenty-mile swelter after a wounded bison even in the hottest weather. An unerring shot, he was known to calmly await the furious onset of a tiger till the brute was within a few yards, and then lay it low with a ball crashing through its skull. It is even said that, having tracked a noted man-eater to its lair, he disdained to shoot at the sleeping brute, but roused it with a stone and then shot it as it was making at him open-mouthed. He was known to decline to take part in beats for game or to use an elephant to shoot from, but would always go alone save for his factotum Yalloo, and would follow up the most dangerous game on foot. He was a man of few words and it was with the greatest difficulty he could be got to talk of his adventures. When pressed to relate an incident in which it was known that he had done a deed of the utmost daring, he would dismiss the subject with half-a-dozen words, generally : "Yes, the beast came at me, and I shot him." Yalloo was as loquacious as his master was reticent, and it was through his glibness of tongue round the camp fire, that much of Gordon Cumming's *shikar* doings became known. Yalloo believed absolutely in his master and would follow him anywhere. "He carries two deaths in his hand and can place them where he likes (alluding to his master's accuracy with the rifle) ; therefore, why should I fear ? Has a beast two lives that I should dread him ? A single shot is enough, and even a *Rakshasha* (giant demon) would lie low."

A Deputy Commissioner in the Mysore service, Cumming was posted at Shimoga, in the north-west of the province, when he heard of the doings of

Peer Bux at Hunsur, and obtained permission to try and bag him. He soon heard all the *khubber* (news) as to the habits of the brute, and he determined to systematically stalk him down. For this purpose he established three or four small camps at various points in the districts ravaged by the brute, so that he might not be hampered with a camp following him about but could call in at any of the temporary shelters he had put up and get such refreshment as he required. He knew it would be a work of days, perhaps weeks, following up the tracks of the rogue, who was here to-day and twenty miles off to-morrow; but he had confidence in his own staying powers, and he trusted to the chapter of lucky accidents to cut short a toilsome stalk.

Selecting the banks of the Kabbany as the most likely place to fall in with the tracks of Peer Bux, he made Karkankote his resting-place for the time, while a careful examination was made of the ground on the left bank of the river. Tracks were soon found, but these always led to the river, where they were lost, and no further trace of them was found on either bank. He learned from the Kurambas that the elephant was in the habit of entering the river and floating down for a mile or so before it made for the banks. As it travelled during the night and generally laid up in dense thicket during the day, there was some chance of coming up with it, if only the more recent tracks could be followed up uninterruptedly; but with the constant breaks in the scent whenever the animal took to the water he soon saw that tracking would be useless in such country, and that he must shift to where there were no large streams. A couple of weeks had been spent in the arduous work of following up the brute from Karkankote to Frazerpett and back again to the river near Hunsur and then on to Heggadavencotta. Even the tireless Yalloo now became wearied and began to doubt the good fortune of his master. Yet Gordon Cumming was as keen as ever, and would not give up his plan of following like a sleuth-hound on the tracks of the brute. On several occasions they had fallen in with other parties out on the same errand as themselves, but these contented themselves with lying in wait at certain points the brute was known to frequent. These parties had invariably asked Gordon Cumming to join them, as they pronounced his stern chase a wildgoose one and said he was as likely to come up with the Flying Dutchman as he was with the Terror of Hunsur.

It was getting well into the third week of this long chase, when the tracks led through some scrub jungle which would not give cover to anything larger than a spotted deer. They had come on to the ruins of an ancient village, the only signs of which were a small temple fast falling into decay, and an enormous banyan tree (*Ficus religiosa*). It was midday; the heat was intense, and they sat under the shade of the tree for a little rest. Cumming was munching a biscuit, while Yalloo was chewing a little *pan* (betel-leaf), when a savage scream was heard and there, not twenty paces off, was the Terror of Hunsur coming down on them in a terrific charge. From the position in which Cumming was sitting a fatal shot at the elephant was almost impossible, as it carried its head high and only its chest was exposed. A shot there might rake the body without touching lungs or heart, and then the brute would be on him. Without the least sign of haste and with the utmost unconcern Gordon Cumming still seated, flung his *sola topee* (sun hat) at the beast when it was about ten yards from him. The rogue stopped momentarily to examine this strange object, and lowered its head for the purpose. This was exactly what Cumming wanted, and quick as thought a bullet, planted in the centre of the prominence just above the trunk, crashed through its skull, and the Terror of Hunsur dropped like a stone, shot dead. "Ah, comrade," said Yalloo, when relating the story, "I could have kissed the Bahadoor's (my lord's) feet when I saw him put the gun down, and go on eating his biscuit just as if he had only shot a bird of some kind, instead of that devil of an elephant. I was ready to die of fright; yet here was the *Sahib* sitting down as if his life had not been in frightful jeopardy just a moment before. Truly, the *Sahibs* are great!"

GORDON CUMMING SHOOTING THE "TERROR OF HUNSUR."

[*To face page* 62.

AN ADVENTURE WITH A BOA.

SAMOO, my Jhora boatman, is the finest story-teller I know. He is a man of few words, but with appropriate gesture and imitation he paints such a word-picture that you can fancy the scene enacted before you. He is no traveller—has never been twenty miles from his native village—yet he has had strange experiences, and strangest of the many is his adventure with a boa.

I might have been inclined to doubt the accuracy of his description of the great snake's method of fight if it were not for the singular confirmation it receives from Rudyard Kipling's work, "The Jungle Book," in which an account is given of the serpent Kaa's fight with the *bander-logue* (monkeys).

As I cannot give Samoo's gesture and imitation, I must endeavour to paraphrase them.

"It was in the rains, *Huzoor* (your worship), three years ago, when the Koel was in flood. I was fishing at the *gagra* (rapids). When the water is muddy we can only fish with the rod and line, and then we only get small cat-fish. These fish take bait readily in flood time, and I was seated behind a large rock fishing in a pool above the rapids when a rustling in the long grass, some twenty yards above stream, attracted my attention. It seemed as if a herd of bullocks were rushing down to the stream. Then I heard splash! splash! and ough! two huge snakes, from ten to fifteen cubits long and as thick as my thigh, entered the water. I felt great fright and could not run, but crouched behind the stone and looked. Whether they were fighting or merely gambolling I cannot tell. They twined their bodies round one another and raised themselves higher than a man out of the water, and fell with a great crash. This they did several times, and then one—the smaller of the two—unloosed itself from the coil of the other and swam to the opposite shore, where I lost sight of it. Its mate, after swimming once or twice round the pool, came out on the bank near where it entered the water, and stretched itself beside a log of *sal* (wood) which was lying on the sands. So well did it conceal itself that not a vestige of it was to be seen, and had I not seen it creep beside the log I should not have known there was so large a snake there. I waited some time, and then was about to steal off home when I heard a shrill squeal, followed by a succession of grunts, in the forest behind me. The snake also seemed to have heard the sounds, for when I next looked at him his head was resting flat on the log and his body drawn up in zigzags behind him. The log was lying across the mouth of a small water-course leading to the river, and down this water-course the sounds were fast approaching. A wild pig rushed out of the water-course and made for the river. Just as it was leaping over the log the snake darted forward and coiled itself round the body and neck of the pig, and held it fast. The pig gave a struggle or two and was dead. The snake had its coil still round the body of the pig, when out rushed a pack of wild dogs which were evidently hunting the pig. The foremost dog was nearly on to the snake before it saw him. With a sharp yell it sprang to one side, while the boa uncoiled itself from the pig and hissing loudly sheltered itself behind the log. The whole pack now formed themselves up behind their leader, snarling savagely and showing their teeth and eyeing the carcase of the pig the while. But the snake was not to be baulked of his prey. His body was close-drawn in great folds near to his head, which was only just raised off the ground; his eyes gleaming and his forked tongue flickering in and out of his closed lips, while the end of his tail kept swaying from side to side, as hiss after hiss replied to the snarls of the dogs. This went on for a little while, until one of the dogs made a snap at the pig. Quicker than an arrow from a well-strung bow, shot forward the head of the snake, full six feet, and struck the venturesome dog straight in the ribs, and was back to its original position in a moment. The dog was thrown clean off its legs several paces, and with a convulsive kick or two was dead. You smile, *Huzoor*, but it is true words I am telling. These snakes always fight in that way. I have seen a bullock's ribs broken by a blow from the head of a boa. The boa has a square nose, like that of a buffalo, and it is not soft, but hard and bony, and it can deliver a blow as hard as that of twenty men together, and strike an object eight feet away. Seeing one of their number killed, the dogs now took counsel together and settled on a plan of action. They formed a complete circle round the snake and kept trotting round and round. One would then make a feint of attacking the snake, and when he launched forth to strike his adversary, another dog would rush from the opposite side and drive its teeth into the great snake's body. This ruse answered admirably for a time, and the snake began to bleed profusely from several severe wounds, and I was expecting a speedy victory for the dogs, when the boa, grown more wary, declined to be drawn by the feigned attack, but reserved himself for the dog that actually seized him, and again despatched it with a single blow of his formidable head. Several dogs were killed in this way, when the whole pack rushed on him at once, and tried to seize him by the head. As well try to seize a rat in a hut. The head was here, there, and everywhere. Ough! bah! bah! it was a sight. The snarls of the dogs, the hiss of the snake, the yelps of the dying dogs! It was all over in a moment; only three dogs were left, and these took to flight. The snake glided back to its old position behind the log, and seemed to go to sleep. After a time I crept cautiously away and went to my village. Several of us came down in our boats in the evening.

We threw stones at the log, but there was no snake there. On landing we found the bodies of the pig and eight dogs. The snake had crept away into the forest. We saw his tracks marked with blood, but were afraid to follow. The Sonthals from Godamarree ate the pig; the dogs we threw into the river."

Such is Samoo's tale, told in fewer words but far less graphically. How much truth there is in it I cannot say, but the villagers all believe it to be true. One can well conceive the enormous force of a blow delivered with the tremendous power of the mass of muscle making up the body of these great serpents. But the question remains, "Do boas strike such blows with the head?" Mr. Kipling asserts it in his "Jungle Book," and now Samoo tells the same tale. The generally-accepted belief is that pythons always use their power of constriction to crush and kill their prey. I have myself seen a nine-foot rock snake thus kill a large-sized goat, but Samoo and other natives assert that boas merely use their constrictive power to break the bones and squeeze the body of their prey into a shape fit to swallow, but that they first kill it with a blow of the head.

THE ONE-EYED MAN-EATER.

Some years ago I was engaged in prospecting for gold on the north-west-frontier of Mysore, between the districts of Chittaldroog and Shimoga. The forest tracts of Ubrani and Gangur, where my work lay, are made up of stunted growths of bamboo, babul and date-palm—a very desolate country, the villages being few and far between and the cultivation limited to the margins of the few streams that drain this hilly region. This portion of the country had a very evil reputation, for it was said to be infested with tigers, which found ready shelter in the low thorny jungle seen all over these hills. At the time of my visit a notorious man-eater was ravaging the country around Gangur, and it was reported that twenty-six human victims had fallen a prey to the savage monster in the past six months. A large reward had been offered for his slaughter by the Mysore Government, and some of the most noted native *shikaris* had been after him but had failed to bag the cunning brute. Several parties of British officers from the military stations of Bangalore and Belgaum had also been after him, and although a number of other tigers had been shot, the famous man-eater was still at large. There could be no mistaking him. He was said to have but one eye, the other having been knocked out by a native when out duck-shooting on the Sulikeray tank (a large artificial lake in this neighbourhood). The man's story was that he was perched in the fork of a large tree on the margin of the lake, waiting for daylight in order to shoot the wild geese which frequent this tank. At daybreak he noticed an enormous tiger go down to the lake to drink. It then came and stretched itself under the very tree on which he was perched. After a time it appeared to go to sleep, with its head between its paws. He had only small shot in his single-barrel fowling-piece, but he thought at this short range he might be able to kill the brute, and the Government reward of thirty-five rupees for a tiger appeared to be within his grasp. He took careful aim at its eye and fired, dropping his gun at the same time in his agitation. With a fearful roar the tiger rushed away, tearing the bark from the trees with his teeth in his savage fury. After the lapse of some considerable time, and when the sun was well up in the heavens, the man got off his perch and made his way as quickly as he could to his village. The next day a careful search was made for the tiger, but nothing was seen of him. A few weeks later a man was carried off from the path between Uhrani and Gangur and partially eaten by the tiger. This happened again, and then it became a common occurrence, not a week passing but a human being was carried off. The brute seemed to frequent the high road between the district stations of Chittaldroog and Shimoga, and so daring had he become that all traffic between these two towns was at a stand-still for the time. He had been seen several times by villagers and goat-herds, and the loss of one of his eyes was noted. Probably it was this very loss of an eye that led him to take to man-eating, as when wounded he would have been unable to roam far in search of his natural prey, and driven by hunger to attack man, he found him so easy a victim that thenceforth he hunted man instead of beast. He had been known to carry off a cartman and leave the bullocks from an ox-waggon conveying goods along the road. Latterly he had taken to killing the *dâk*-men, or native runners who carry the post from station to station in outlying parts of the country. These *dâk* - runners carry the letter-bags slung on a stick thrown over the shoulder. At the further end of the stick is a bunch of small bells which make a kind of rhythmic jangle as the men trot along. The sound of these bells can be heard a considerable way off, and evidently this tiger had learned to associate their tinkle-tinkle with approaching prey. He would lie in wait in some unfrequented corner and then pounce on the unfortunate *dâk*-runner as he passed with the mails. Four poor wretches had fallen in succession to the maw of the fearful creature, and none would now venture to carry the mails.

I had with me as my assistant a young Cornishman named Provis, out from England for the first time. We had pitched our camp at a wayside overseer's bungalow, about ten miles from the village of Gangur and on the Chittaldroog side. The country was open for several miles on all sides of the bungalow, the forest beginning some four miles west, where the road descended a kind of *ghât* (hill-side) into the valley leading to the Badra river. It was this spot that the man-eater was said chiefly to frequent, although his range extended to villages many miles away. Owing to four *dâk*-men having been carried off by the tiger we could not get our letters from the nearest postal station, but had to ride in ourselves once a week to Shimoga, forty miles off. None of our servants nor the villagers dared to go alone any distance from the bungalow. Provis had heard and read so much of tiger-shooting that he was eager to have a pot at the tiger, all the more so from the fact of its being a man-eater, for great would be the kudos should he bag him. We scoured the country for miles, doing our prospecting at the same time, but never got sight of the tiger. We sat out night after night in a *machan* in all the most likely places, with a fine buffalo as a bait; yet no tiger came. When we were at Gangur we heard of him at Ubrani; when we got there, he had "killed" at some village ten miles off. We should have grown sceptical as to the existence of the tiger if it were not for the gruesome sight of the partially-eaten body of a young woman taken from the fields in broad daylight at a village seven miles from our camp If we could have induced the poor weeping relatives to leave the body where it was found, we might probably have got a shot at the monster on his return to complete his meal. But we had not the heart to urge it on them, when they wished to remove what was left of their kinswoman for burial. We gave them sufficient money to bury their dead and drown their sorrow in arrack, and turned away heart-sick at the ghastly spectacle we had just witnessed, vowing that we would not relax our efforts to rid the place of the brute.

Talking over the events of the day at the bungalow, Provis suggested that if one of us disguised himself as a *dâk*-man and carried the bells over his shoulder and trudged the bit of *ghât* road where the tiger had carried off the four *dâk*-men, while the other perched himself in a *machan* just near the spot where the tiger had made his previous attacks, we might probably get a shot at him. He thought that even if nothing came of it, the attempt would still serve to hearten the natives and show them that *dâk*-running was not so dangerous after all. This last argument, the inconvenience we had ourselves suffered from the stoppage of the post together with the need of a little excitement in our hum-drum life, induced me to consent to his proposal. No thought of danger ever entered my mind for the moment. The toss of a rupee soon decided that I was to enact the *dâk*-man and Provis do the shooting from the *machan*. We sat up long, talking over the details of our mad-cap scheme, and probably dreamt of it that night. Next morning we got together a number of villagers, and set off for the scene of the night's operations. The news of our plot to circumvent Master Stripes soon got wind, and the whole male population of the village assembled to help to erect the *machan*. Half-way down the declivity was a large tree which overhung the road at the angle of a zig-zag. In order to cut off this corner the natives took a short cut across the zig-zag. This path was worn into deep ruts, and it was along these ruts that the tiger concealed himself when lying in wait for the *dâk*-men. From the *machan* in the tree the roadway on both sides, as well as the short cut, could be plainly seen. Provis was to ride over at four o'clock in the afternoon and conceal himself in the *machan*. I was to ride over at about six, dismount some distance away from the edge of the jungle, send the pony back and then begin my experience as a *dâk*-man. Nothing would induce our *syces* (grooms) to remain with the ponies anywhere near the *ghât*, so we arranged to walk back to the bungalow after our adventure. Prompt to the hour Provis set out and ensconced himself in the *machan*, taking with him our whole battery of two double-barrel smooth-bores and a Snider carbine. Meanwhile I got myself up in a dark serge suit, *shikar* shoes, a white cummerbund and turban, and, provided with a stout staff and bells to complete my personation of a native post-runner, I set off amid the plaudits of the natives, who assembled in crowds to witness this escapade of the *pitheya dorays* (mad gentlemen). It was just dusk when I got to within a mile of the head of the *ghât*. A bright moon was soon shining, so objects were clear enough. I dismounted and sent back my pony and began my tramp towards the jungle, shaking my bells as I went. I had two miles in all to go before reaching the *machan*. The first mile was in comparatively open ground; after that the forest deepened and but little of the roadway could be seen. I had started my tramp in a careless mood, thinking more of my ludicrous disguise than of any danger to myself. As I descended the declivity I began to realise my position. Supposing the tiger actually attacked me, what was I to do? I was wholly unarmed with the exception of the wooden staff, but what was that when matched against a tiger! I felt more than half-inclined to turn back and concoct some tale as to my return. But what of Provis? Could I shout to him from where I was? Might not this very shouting attract the tiger? To turn back then was perhaps as dangerous as to go forward, for the tiger might already be behind me. A glance backward sent a cold shiver all over me, and I set off at a sharp trot to join Provis. The jingling of the bells seemed to reassure me, and I went along for a few hundred yards. Suddenly I came to a stop, my heart beating furiously. There was a dark object standing by the road. The tiger! Should I run from it? My sudden stopping evidently alarmed the beast and it scampered off into the jungle, with the unmistakable lope of a jackal.

I cannot recollect what happened in the next few minutes, but I found myself under the *machan* and Provis shouting, "What on earth has scared you, old man? Did you see the tiger?" A strong nip from Provis's flask and I was able to give some garbled account of having been out of wind with the trot. Shouldering our guns we walked down the *ghât* and then back to camp, but saw no signs of the tiger. Several times that night I got up with a feeling of the "creeps," and imagined I was being stalked by the man-eater.

Next morning Provis insisted that we must make another attempt, this time changing places. No argument of mine would alter his determination. "If you don't come, old man, I go alone and do the *dâk*-man. I won't have the natives say that the *chick doray* (little gentleman) is afraid." I tried to persuade him to take one of the double guns with him; but no, he would go just as I went. Well, I got into the *machan* at 5 o'clock and made a nice little opening on three sides, so as to rest my gun and command the road on both sides, as well as the short cut. After that I sat down to wait quietly but found it a most difficult matter, as at dusk the mosquitoes got scent of me and kept me on the move trying to beat them away from my ears. At last I heard the bells in the distance, when it occurred to me that should anything happen to Provis I would be seriously to blame. I ought at any cost to have dissuaded him from his rash attempt. Every tinkle of the bells I feared would be the last, and it was with the utmost relief that at length I saw his figure looming in the distance. Now he has left the main road and got into the short cut. He is still about two hundred yards off, when—Merciful Heaven! What is that I see stealing along some thirty yards behind him? The ruts hide it from view for a moment, but there it is again. There is no mistaking that huge head. It is the tiger! The bright moonlight shows up his yellow body between the little ridges in the road, as crouching low he stealthily follows my friend, actually stalking him. I was in an agony of nervous tremor. Should I shout to warn Provis? But that would probably cause him to stop, and the tiger would be on to him. Every moment seemed an age, yet there was my friend in the jaws of death and yet wholly unconscious of his extreme danger. Could I but stay the shaking of my hands there was a chance yet, as I could depend on my Snider for anything up to a hundred yards. I aimed as best I could at the tiger, but those who have done tiger-shooting know how small a mark this great brute offers when, crouched low, he steals along after his prey. He was visibly lessening the distance between himself and Provis, and would probably make his final rush in another moment or two. I aimed at a spot a few yards in advance where the path was comparatively level, so that I would be able to see the whole of the tiger's body, and immediately he appeared there I fired. Provis stopped a moment; then rushed forward exclaiming, "D——n it, old man, stop that; your bullet pinged within an inch of my ear! Don't crack jokes in that way!" "Hurry up! hurry up, for God's sake! There is the tiger after you!" I gasped out; and hastily helped my friend into the *machan* beside me. We then looked out for the brute, but could see nothing of him. I felt sure of my shot, and declared he must be dead or dying behind one of the ruts. Provis was thoroughly scared when I told him of his narrow escape; and we both vowed we would never attempt tiger-shooting in that manner again. After waiting a quarter of an hour we fired several shots into the air. Waiting an hour and hearing nothing, we again discharged our pieces and then, re-loading carefully, descended and walked to where I last saw the tiger; but there was no tiger there. Feeling quite sure that we would recover him in the morning, we walked home and received quite an ovation from the natives when I told them that their arch-enemy was slain. Next morning we carefully searched the ground; but although the mark where my bullet struck the ground and glanced off and the marks of Provis's shoes were distinct, there was not the slightest trace of a tiger's pug anywhere about. To this day I cannot be sure whether it was a tiger I fired at, or merely a phantom of my heated imagination. That the tiger was not dead we had sickening evidence a week later, when the head, arms and legs of a man were brought to us. The poor fellow had been killed the previous day at Ubrani, and the remnants of the tiger's meal were brought us to view, as a silent reproach for our want of success. Four months later, the one-eyed man-eater was shot by a native in his betel-garden and brought into Shimoga. There was no mistaking the brute, as one eye was completely gone. He was an enormous animal, of a fine bright yellow—certainly with the finest skin I have ever seen.

———

MY *SHIKAREE* FRIENDS.

II.—LUTCHMAN THE BEYDAR.

WHEN in the sixteenth century the confederate Mussulman forces under Adil Shah, the monarch of Goolburga, defeated the Hindoo sovereign of Vijianuggar at the decisive battle of Talikot, and thus finally overthrew the last of the Hindoo kingdoms of South India, it was noticed that the utmost efforts of the brilliant Mussulman cavalry could make no impression on a body of Hindoo infantry which kept the field when all around was rout and slaughter. "Who," asked Adil Shah, "are those brave spearsmen?" "*Beytars* (huntsmen)," replied his attendants. "Nay, rather *Beydars* (without fear)," said the chivalrous Mussulman sovereign. "Henceforth they shall be known, not as *Beytars* (huntsmen), but as *Beydars* (the fearless)." This punning title of *Beydar Beytar* (the fearless huntsmen) is still borne by the clansmen of the famous caste of huntsmen inhabiting North Mysore and parts of the Southern Mahratta country. Under their *Palegars*, or tribal chiefs, they formed the flower of that Mysore army which, under Hyder Ali, struck terror into the hearts of the Governor and Council of Fort St. George, and set at defiance the united efforts of the English, the Nizam, and the Mahrattas for twenty years. The ruthless proselytizing of the bigoted Tipu alienated these brave clansmen and turned them into bitter foes, and thus hastened the destruction of that mighty kingdom which his father Hyder had founded with their help.

Under British rule this once famous soldiery have settled down into peaceful cultivators, but they still retain much of their traditional habits as huntsmen, and at stated intervals assemble in large numbers and organise a regular battue of all the game in their neighbourhood. Armed with short stabbing spears they will fearlessly meet the raging wild boar in full career, and with a well-planted stab nearly sever the shoulder from the body of the brute, while they leap nimbly aside to avoid its formidable tusks, still retaining hold of the spear, which they never throw. A favourite weapon with which they kill hare, jackals, and birds of all kinds is the *kirasoo*, or curled stick, a kind of Indian boomerang. The *kirasoo* is made from the ironwood shrub, common all over Mysore. It is a spiral stick about three feet long, and ending in a knob. Its weight varies from eight to twelve ounces. There are two methods of throwing the *kirasoo*, and in both the narrow end is held in the hand, the knob being forward. If an object on the ground is aimed at, the *kirasoo* is thrown under-arm with a jerk, its flight being straight with a screw motion. Immediately the knob strikes the ground the curled portion swings over it, describing a circle. The knob now jerks away a few feet and another circle is described, and so on a series of loops or circles are made by the stick until finally it falls to rest. Any hare or jackal within a range of several yards from the spot where the knob first touches the ground is almost certain to be knocked down by the stick in its gyrations. If thrown among a lot of birds the weapon does great damage. I have seen as many as six quail killed with a single throw. The other method of throwing the *kirasoo* is far more difficult and requires very considerable skill. The stick is swung round the head several times, and then launched forward. After a straight flight of about twenty yards it makes a series of zig-zags upwards and then drops. Among a flock of pigeons in flight this does great execution, killing and maiming many.

My friend Lutchman, the Beydar, was an expert with the curled stick, and would do far more execution with it among the birds than I with my double-barrelled shot-gun. Innumerable blue rock pigeons take up their abode in the old pits and shafts of the ancient gold-workings seen on the auriferous tracts in Mysore. The mouths of these shafts are generally concealed by scrubby thorn bushes. Our method was to approach as quietly as possible, and when within a few yards to throw some stones, when out would fly a great flock of birds. Bang! bang! would go both my barrels, and whizz went Lutchman's *kirasoo;* we each secured our bag, but Lutchman's nearly always exceeded mine. When I extolled his skill and pointed to his larger number of birds, he would modestly remark: "My lord and father shoots for pleasure, I kill for a living; if my lord hunted for a living, how great would be the load!"

Lutchman was a fine specimen of a native athlete. About five feet four inches in height, with clean cut features, a straight nose, and small flexible nostrils, he would be considered a good-looking man anywhere. Well-shaped limbs, small hands and feet, slim waist and sloping shoulders, he could outrun all the men of his village, whether in a short sprint or a five-mile race; while at lifting weights he was not far behind our stalwart North Country and sturdy Cornish miners. Unlike most of his clansmen Lutchman was a Lingayet by religion, and he wore the Phallic emblem in a little silver box on his right arm. Before starting on an expedition of any kind, before beginning a race or putting the stone, even before beginning his day's work, he would touch the *lingam* on his right arm with his left hand, and then touch his forehead—this being his method of asking a blessing on his undertaking. A small section of the Beydars are Lingayets; the great bulk of them worship the sanguinary goddess Kali. Tipu Sultan forcibly seized a number of Beydars and had them circumcised, hoping in this way to convert them to Mahomedanism; but the infuriated tribesmen rose in rebellion, and retiring into their strong hill-fortresses, or droogs, bid defiance to

Tipu and all his hosts. They were besieged for years in the famous fort of Chitaldroog, and although at times reduced to the utmost extremities, a bold sally on more than one occasion enabled them to seize the enemy's camp and re-victual the fortress. It is said that on the capture of Chitaldroog by treachery, there were found several thousand human heads before the shrine of the goddess Kali within the fort. During the siege, at daybreak each day, the collary horn—a long brazen trumpet used by these tribes—would sound, and out would rush a number of Beydars from the most unexpected quarters, and kill and behead such of the enemy as fell into their hands. These heads were offered as a morning sacrifice to the sanguinary goddess.

Wild boar hunting is the chief sport among the Beydars. In the luxuriant millet fields and canebrakes of the Mysore table-land this brute attains an enormous size. When the millet is in ear and the cane ripens, a sounder of pig will do an immense amount of damage in a single night. The path taken by the swine in their course from their haunts to the fields is carefully marked, and a day for the hunt is selected when the moon shines bright towards morn. At that hour the herds have finished feeding and make for their haunts. The most skilful among the spearsmen post themselves on each side of the path the pigs take when returning. A leafy branch resting on the ground and supported by the left hand, conceals the spearsman. In his right hand is held the short stabbing spear, with its keen blade nearly a foot long and four inches wide. The whole of the inhabitants of the village, men, women and children, with all the village curs, surround the fields, leaving open only the path that the animals use. At a given signal the men shout, women and children scream, dogs bark and the whole make such a din that the frightened swine at once bolt for the jungle. The sows and pigs first break cover, and are allowed to pass the foremost spearsmen, to be despatched by the less skilful huntsmen behind. Now a large black object looms in the distance and trots slowly up the path, stopping now and again to turn and give a grunt of defiance. To my friend Lutchman has been assigned the place of honour—the foremost spear. A bright gleam in his eye and a rising of the muscles of his arms alone show that he is all alert. A shower of stones from behind, thrown by lads concealed for the purpose, sends the huge brute up the path at a gallop, his jaws champing furiously the while. Now he approaches the branch held by Lutchman. A bright gleam of steel, a shrill scream of rage and pain, and the boar stumbles forward a few paces in his death throes, his shoulder nearly severed from his body by the well-planted thrust and upward jerk of Lutchman's spear. A shout of "*Shabash! shabash!!* (Well done! well done!!)" rings out from his brother hunters, and Lutchman, the hero of the hour, proceeds to plant his foot on the body of his fallen foe and declare himself "the lord of the wild boar" (a favourite title of honour among these people), amid the plaudits of his companions. The boar is carried in triumph to the village, where an equal division is made of the flesh, the head being the perquisite of his slayer. Lutchman has the tusks of many boars in his hut; some of these are quite five inches long and must have belonged to hoary monsters. Yet he never boasts of his prowess, and even when asked to tell the tale of his victories, he merely says, "The foolish animal rushed on my spear, thinking it was a millet stalk, but he was mistaken."

A MAN-EATING WOLF.

An Engineer in the Public Works Department, India, who has had much experience of India lately told me that he thought none of the wild beasts of that country were equal to the wolf in savage ferocity, wanton destructiveness and wild daring. He has spent much of his life in the North-West Provinces and Oude, where wolves are very plentiful, and he has often had occasion to remember that there are other animals in India as dangerous as the man-eating tiger and even more destructive to human life.

On one occasion, while engaged on some bridge-work at Sheegottee, near Gya on the Grand Trunk Road, the native watchmen set to guard a brick-field were so frequently carried off by a pair of wolves that at last no one would remain after dark anywhere near the brick-kilns. One incident that my friend related well exemplifies the daring of these brutes. A watchman's hut had been erected near the brick-fields, and two men were appointed as care-takers. One moonlight night they were sleeping in the verandah of the hut, and, as natives of India generally do, they slept with their cloths drawn over their heads.

One of the men was awakened by a gurgling noise and a sound of struggling. On looking up he saw that a large wolf had seized his brother-watchman by the throat, and was endeavouring to drag him off, while a second wolf was sitting on its haunches calmly watching the proceedings from outside. He at once got hold of his *lathie* (quarter-staff), and began belabouring the wolf, but it was only after repeated blows that it loosened its hold; and then it only went off a few yards and kept growling and showing its teeth. Fortunately the watchman was a brave fellow, and a man of resource. The fire had not yet gone out, and tearing a wisp of grass from the thatched roof, he lighted it and rushed at the wolves with the flaming firebrand, thus putting them to flight, as there is nothing the wolf dreads so much as flaming fire. He had now time to attend to his companion, who had fainted away. There were several slight wounds in the neck, but the thick cloth the man had drawn over him had prevented the wolf from seizing him by the throat, the spot for which these animals always make, and dragging him away.

Some years ago I was camped near the village of Sat-bowrie (Seven Wells) on the high-road from Nagpore to Jubbulpore. The village had an unenviable notoriety for thieves and was more frequently called Chor-bowrie (Thieves' Wells) than Sat-bowrie. The hill ranges to the north were inhabited by a wild race known as Bheels, the most expert thieves in the world, and a number of these Bheels had settled round Sat-bowrie, and were known to be concerned in the numerous robberies that had recently taken place in that neighbourhood. A special officer—Lieutenant Cumberledge, I think, of the Thuggi Department—had been sent down to investigate, as several persons had disappeared from the village of late and it was thought that the Thugs (professional stranglers) had had something to do with their disappearance, as the bodies were not recovered and these wretches were known to be particularly skilful in hiding away the corpses of their victims.

Cumberledge told me a strange story. His first search was for signs of Thugs, but no strangers were known to be about nor had parties of seemingly respectable Hindoo travellers (the usual disguise of Thugs) gone up or down the road. He then thought that the murderers might be Bheels; but Bheels were also among the missing persons, and a great fear had fallen on their people, as they ascribed the disappearance of their fellows to a malignant spirit. Robbery evidently was not an object, since most of those who had disappeared were poor people with few or no ornaments. The officer then imagined that the cause of all this mischief might be a man-eating tiger; but he soon had to dismiss that idea from his mind, as no tiger pugs had been seen, and the keenest trackers had been unable to find traces of one of these brutes anywhere in the neighbourhood. A man-eating wolf then suggested itself, as it was known that wolves frequently took to man-eating, and then became very daring. The circumstances attending the mysterious disappearances were very like the work of a man-eating wolf, as the victims—if victims they were—always vanished at night; they were generally taken from the verandah of their huts, and not a bone of the unfortunates was found. The tiger will usually leave the larger bones of the creatures he preys on; wolves will not leave a vestige, as they are more fond of bones than even dogs are. But even this reasoning appeared to be at fault, for at first no trace of any creature's foot-marks could be found. Eventually, however, near to some of the houses from which people had disappeared, there was seen the trail of some animal which no one could recognise. It certainly was not the track of any known animal, and the Bheels and local *shikaris* regarded it as "uncanny," and ascribed it to a wood-demon or *rakshasha*. Four rounded holes, with a brush-like mark before and behind, were all that could be seen, and these disappeared sometimes in places where distinct trail should have been found. Cumberledge was nonplussed, and told me his tale with much chagrin. He had been a fortnight on the spot and was no nearer the solution of the mystery than when he arrived. Indeed, he admitted to me that he was more puzzled now than when he first came, as the ideas he had formed on the subject had had to be abandoned one by one, and he was now further off than ever from scenting a trail. Two persons were missing since his arrival on the spot: one the wife of the village herdsman, taken from inside her hut; the other a youth of seventeen, last seen sleeping before the village shop in the heart of the hamlet. He asked me if I would join him in the endeavour to unearth this strange mystery, and as I expected to be in that neighbourhood for a month I readily consented.

About a week after this a child was taken from a Bheel's hut some distance from the village. The child was said to be sleeping in its mother's arms at the time. She heard a rustle during the night and, getting up, missed the child. Thinking that it had crawled away, she searched round the hut and, not finding it, gave the alarm. She found the bamboo door partly pushed aside, so knew that some animal had entered. Not a trace was to be seen on the hard-beaten clay in front of the hut, only a drop or two of blood showed that the poor infant had been carried away by some brute. We felt sure now that this night's work at least was done by a wolf, as both Cumberledge and I had heard of cases of wolves stealing into houses at night and taking sleeping children from their mother's arms without awakening the parent. We scouted the country for miles round, using several good dogs in the search, without any result. Two days afterwards the lieutenant's servant came to me early in the morning and said his master wished to see me, as the Demon had come to the village in the night and had carried off the *sonar* (goldsmith). He knew it was the Demon, as his marks were plainly to be seen in the roadway. When I got there I found a large crowd collected near the goldsmith's house, but they were carefully kept away from the vicinity of some well-marked signs in the dust before the house. They were similar to the marks seen near other houses from which inmates had been taken — four rounded holes, about fifteen inches apart and placed two and two together. The back holes were much wider than those in front, and from these latter a slight depression extended for about ten inches terminating in a knuckle mark. A similar knuckle mark was seen behind each of the near holes, but further away, and the longitudinal mark was wanting. My attention was drawn to these peculiarities by Cumberledge, whose training as a police officer qualified him for taking note of signs that others would have overlooked. The natives were loud in their expressions of opinion as to the machinations of a forest demon. One old man indeed declared that he had seen the evil thing. It first appeared as an old man, and then changed into a dog, and then vanished. His story, though laughed at by us, was firmly believed by the simple villagers, and after-events proved that there was some truth in it. Careful search showed the trail to lead to some stony ground outside the village, where all further trace of it was lost. Returning from an unsuccessful hunt all over the neighbourhood, we came back to the goldsmith's house, with the faint hope of finding some clue, when suddenly a thought struck me that I had seen a similar trail before, and I accordingly told one of the natives present to go down on all fours, knees and elbows on the ground, and crawl for a bit. His tracks gave a fairly good representation, with certain marked differences, of the mysterious track that had puzzled us. "Wolf-boy?" I said to Cumberledge. He was sceptical. "Surely, you don't think a wolf-boy has taken to man-eating? I have heard of such creatures, but I doubt all the stories I have been told of them," he replied. "I don't say we have a man-eating wolf-boy; I merely assert that the tracks have been made by such a creature. I have lately seen one at Seoni, and I noticed that he crawled on his knees and elbows. If you ask a native to go down on all fours, he will either go on his hands and feet or hands and knees; never on his elbows. I noticed this as a peculiarity of the wolf-boy I saw."

On enquiring of the natives whether they had ever heard of or seen a wolf-boy in that neighbourhood, they all had stories to tell of boys being carried away by wolves and brought up by those creatures, but none could personally vouch for having seen one. Numbers of children had been carried off by wolves from their village, but they had been eaten by the beasts. Once, however, the mysterious marks had been cleared up by my explanation, the native *shikaris* appeared to regain all their astuteness. Now that all fear of demons and spirits had vanished, an old Bheel offered to lead us to a ruined temple near to which he had seen similar marks. We bade him lead the way, and we followed. The Bheel took us along some stony ground near to a rivulet about half a mile off. Going down the course about a mile and a half we entered a dense jungle of thorn and brushwood among some hillocks, and at length in a thick clump we saw the ruins of a Sivaite temple. This was carefully surrounded, and guns and spearmen placed in position. The Bheel showed us tracks similar to those already noticed, near the margin of a water-hole in the rivulet, and along a path leading thence to the temple. In addition to these were the well-marked paws of a large wolf. The men were instructed on no account to injure the wolf-boy should he be found, but to capture him alive. The circle gradually narrowed round the old temple, and stones were now thrown among the brushwood to start the game, but without effect. Soon the stone plinth or platform on which these temples are always built was reached, yet no wolf or wolf-boy was to be seen. There was the little chamber in the temple, where the phallic emblem is displayed; the single entrance to this was almost concealed by ruins and brushwood, and was just the kind of place a wolf would select as a den. The *shikaris* were sure we should find the wolves within this lair. Several stones were thrown in, but nothing moved. Now a lighted firebrand was flung in, yet not a sound. Our Bheel guide at last ventured within, with a firebrand in hand, but the place was empty nor was there any sign of its having been frequented by animals of any kind. We turned away in disgust and were just leaving the precincts of the temple when an exclamation from one of the men caused us to return to the platform; and there, adhering to a stone, was a small splash of blood and a little human hair. The splash was recent and evidently made by a body being drawn over the stone. The search was redoubled, but all in vain; not a cranny or nook that would hide a hare was left unprobed.

Sivaite temples are built in the form of a square, for about eight feet of their height, and within this square is the altar or fane. Above the square a four-sided pyramid, highly ornamented, rises to a greater or less height, according to the size of the temple. Archways about eighteen inches high generally pierce the pyramid from side to side. One wall of the square had slightly fallen down at the top, and here also a splash of blood was observed. The men quickly surrounded the temple, and one or two who had mounted the terrace from which the pyramid starts, now announced that the wolf was within the low arch and that a dead body was there also! We were quickly drawn up on the terrace, and there sure enough was the wolf, crouched behind the dead body and snarling viciously. A well-directed shot from Cumberledge killed him on the spot, and one of the Bheels drew out the dead body of the goldsmith, and that of a large-sized female wolf. Not a trace of a wolf-boy was however to be seen anywhere about. The goldsmith's body was only partly eaten, the stomach being nearly gone. The tooth marks in the neck showed how he must have been seized by the wolf and all cry stifled, while death must have been almost instantaneous. The

Bheels pointed to a portion of the arm that was eaten, and said that that had been done by the wolf-boy, as the teeth marks were human. This well might be, for it is well known that when wolf children have been captured and kept in captivity they evince great fondness for raw meat and bones. It was horrible to think of. A careful watch was now set for the wolf-boy; but the story of how he was captured I must reserve for another chapter.

SEEALL, THE WOLF-BOY

Two days after the destruction of the man-eating wolf the Bheel guide and a crowd of followers turned up at our camp late in the evening, with an object swung on a pole and borne by two men. It proved to be the wolf-boy, with wrists and ankles firmly bound together and a pole thrust in between—just as one sees a pig carried about by the natives in country places. Marks of severe handling showed themselves all over his body, and bleeding wounds on several of his captors proved that his teeth and long talons had been freely used. We directed his captors to loose his hands and feet, but they declared he would make off at once if they did so. However, a dog-chain round the waist was all we would permit, and his hands and feet were soon free. Instead of taking to flight he cuddled up hands and feet together, just as children do when asleep. His hair was long, hanging down to his shoulders, and matted in places. It was of a blackish hue with ends of a sandy brown. His legs and arms were thin and sinewy and showed many a scar and bruise; the stomach large and protuberant, the shoulders rounded.

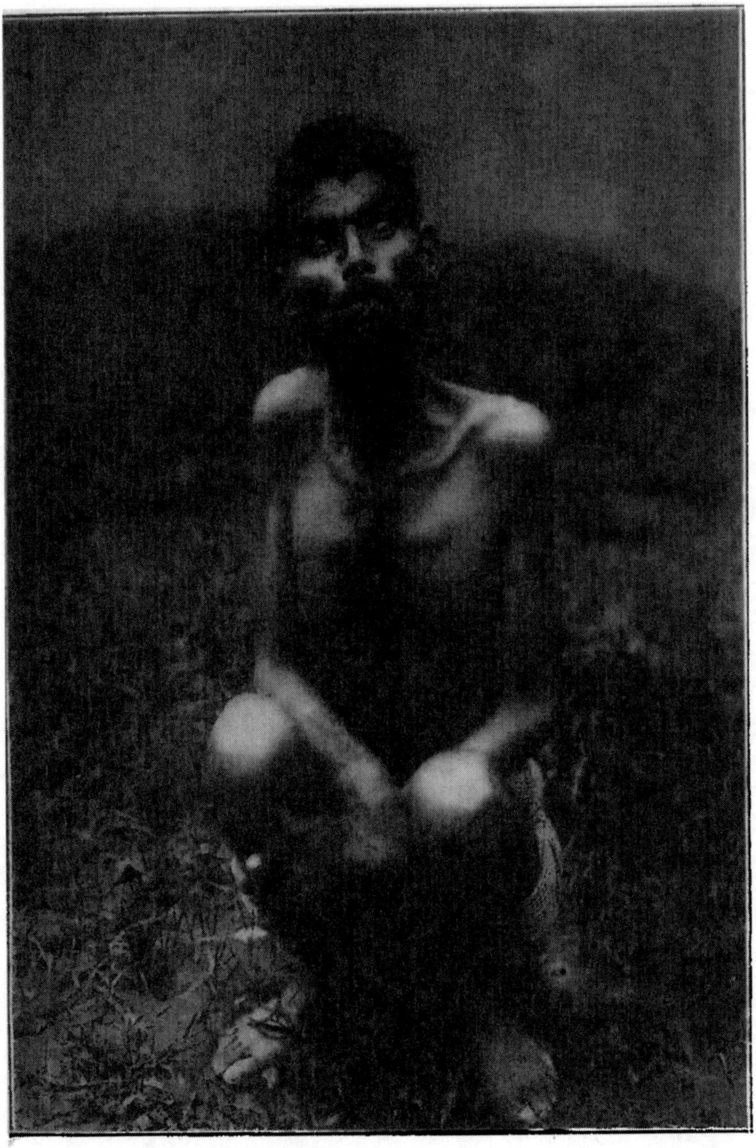

SEEALL, THE WOLF-BOY. (PHOTO TAKEN 10 YEARS AFTER HIS CAPTURE.)

[*To face page* 96.

His teeth were worn to stumps in front, but the canines and molars were well developed. On being given a piece of roast mutton he first smelt it, and then fell to greedily, tearing off pieces with the side of his mouth and swallowing them without mastication. The bone he kept crunching at and gnawing for hours; this explained the worn state of his front teeth. He emitted a strong foxy odour, so that at first even the dogs avoided him, but he appeared to take at once to a large Brinjaree dog of mine, that much resembled a wolf in appearance. When taken into the tent, he showed a great dread of the light, and no persuasion or threats would get him near it. He at once made for a corner, or under the camp stretcher, and coiled himself up. But he was not allowed to stay in the tent as it was found that his hair swarmed with large ticks, and the smell from his body was overpowering. He was therefore given a truss of straw and chained near to the dogs, and a watchman was told off to look after him.

Next morning we were able to examine our strange captive more closely. He was apparently about ten years old. With difficulty we got him to stand upright. He measured four feet one inch in height. His knees, toes, elbows, and the lower part of his palms were hard, and covered with a horny skin, showing that he habitually crawled on knees and elbows. He would occasionally get on to his feet, run a few paces, and then fall on to his palms and hurry along much as one sees a monkey do. When moving he was usually on his elbows and knees. This mode of progression was probably acquired from having to crouch low when entering and leaving the wolf's den. He would not tolerate clothing of any kind nor would he use straw. He preferred to scratch a hole in the sand and cuddle himself up in this. We had his hair close cropped and then took him to the river for a wash, but to this he most strongly objected, and it required all the exertions of two *syces* (grooms) and the *mehter* (sweeper) to force him into the water. We could only get him quiet when Nandair, the Brinjaree dog, was washed beside him. He quite took to the big Brinjaree, but showed a strong aversion to a hairy terrier belonging to Cumberledge.

On being shown the skin of the large she-wolf he became quite excited, smelled at it several times, turned it over, and then uttered the most plaintive howls it has ever been my lot to listen to. They resembled somewhat the first cry of a jackal; hence the servants called him *Seeall* (jackal). After this he would never go near the skin, but showed evident marks of terror when taken near it. He would sleep all day, but became restless at nights, and would then try to escape to the woods. He would not touch dog-biscuits or rice stewed with meat, but would select all the meat and leave the rice. Raw meat he snatched at greedily. He appeared to be particularly partial to the offal of fowls. When on one occasion the cook threw away the entrails of a chicken in his presence, he instantly seized it and swallowed it before anyone could prevent him. He also showed a strong predilection for carrion. His sense of smell was so acute that he could scent a dead cow or buffalo a long distance off, and at once began tugging at his chain to get to it.

Unlike all the other "wolf-boys" of whom we have any record, this creature soon showed he had a great deal of intelligence. He could not speak during the time I knew him, but I was afterwards told he had learnt the Gond language from his keeper and could converse fairly well. In a week's time he was far more intelligent than a dog, and many of his tricks showed that he thought and planned. He would sit by when the dogs were fed, and would remove pieces of meat from the dishes of the other dogs and give them to his particular friend, the great Brinjaree. After a few days we had his head close shaved, and turmeric and oil rubbed well into his skin, and he was then washed with hot water. This treatment soon removed the foxy smell, and the present of a raw chop every day if he kept on his loin-cloth soon induced him to take to clothing. He was an object of great curiosity among the natives, who came in from miles round to see him. All his hair and the parings of his nails, which were abnormally long, were bought by the natives from the *mehter* (sweeper)—in whose charge all private dogs in India are placed, and who therefore took over the care of "Seeall" —and used by them as a remedy for hydrophobia. The women asked permission to worship him, and brought presents of milk and fowls.

With the favour of the "Lord of the Wolves," as they called him, their flocks would, they said, be safe from the ravages of these fierce beasts. But Seeall disliked these offerings of the women, and his eyes would glare so savagely at the sight of the children that several attendants had to watch him at such times to see that he did no mischief. It required no stretch of imagination to believe that he had often shared in a meal, with his wolf companion, off a freshly-killed child, even if he did not himself help to carry off the little victim. The strange disappearance of his trail in the softer parts of the track, noticed in the account of the man-eating wolf, was accounted for by his rising on his feet in such places, and leaving marks undistinguishable from those of other human beings.

The natives declare that when a she-wolf has lost her whelps, from accident or otherwise, she experiences a soreness at the teats from the accumulation of milk, and she then generally steals a child. The sucking of the child relieves the wolf, and the infant is thenceforth regarded as a member of the family and shares the wolves' den and food. When young whelps have been noticed with a wolf-boy, they have always been of a subsequent litter.

When Lieutenant Cumberledge returned to Bhopal, Seeall went with him, and I learnt that he was afterwards sent to a missionary in the North-West. I have reason to believe that he was the original of Rudyard Kipling's *Mowgli*.

BEEMA, THE *BAGH-MAREE* (TIGER-SLAYER).

"I WONDER how you can tolerate such fellows. I would whip them out of the place. They are the curse of all *shikar*, with their cowardly method of killing tigers. There will soon be no tigers left to shoot if you encourage these rascals." So said a planter friend who was staying with me, to whom I had introduced "my friend the *bagh-maree*" (tiger-slayer). Now, I do not in any way share these sentiments, but on the contrary I regard the *bagh-maree* as a most useful member of society. Beema, the *bagh-maree*, has to my knowledge accounted for two panthers, two cheetahs (hunting leopards), one tiger and one bear. Their skins now adorn the verandah of my bungalow. These animals were all killed within a mile of the village of Somij (Chota Nagpore district), and in about two months' time. When it is remembered how vast is the number of cattle and goats annually destroyed by tigers and panthers in India, it will be seen that my friend Beema is anything but deserving of the hard words used by my European *shikaree* friend. In the last twelve months twenty-six head of cattle had been killed within two miles of my bungalow. This of itself is a very serious loss to the villagers, whose chief means of subsistence is agriculture, for which cattle are essential; and if Beema had not thus come to their assistance several families of *ryots* (cultivators) would probably have been ruined.

So much to establish the claims to gentle treatment of my friend the tiger-slayer; and now for his story:—

"I was not always a *bagh-maree*, *Huzoor* (Sir). I am a *tantee* (weaver) by caste. But a *chota bagh* (panther) did it. It made me a *bagh-maree*. It was not a tiger at all; it was a witch that had entered the body of a tiger, to do me an injury. I paid Gagee the Gond two rupees for a charm, and after three years I killed it. *Huzoor*, you know that I killed it behind your *bawarchee-khana* (kitchen) the day after it had killed and eaten Madho's son last year. I know the animal to be the witch by the piece out of its ear which I cut off with my *bulloova* (battle-axe) three years ago at Bara, my village. Gagee the Gond made the charm out of that piece of its ear, and I have the charm yet. Here it is, and there (pointing to the skin on my verandah wall) is the devil. I became a *bagh-maree* out of revenge. You see my head; it is nearly bald, and the girls laugh at me and say I am old, pointing to my baldness, but the witch did that three years ago.

"I made a cloth for an old woman of our village, and charged her one rupee and a half for it. It cost me one rupee two annas worth of cotton thread, so my gain was only six annas. She only paid me Rs. 1–2, and when I pressed for the balance, six annas, she refused to pay, and cursed me, saying a tiger would eat me.

"A few nights after this a *chota bagh* (panther) got into my goat pen and killed two goats and was carrying off a third when I aimed a blow at its head with my axe, but only cut off its ear. It clawed me on the head and the wound caused all the hair to drop off. I vowed revenge and learned how to set the *thair* (spring bow) and poisoned arrows, from Maun Sing the Kowtia. I have been a *bagh-maree* for three years and I have killed two tigers, ten panthers, two hunting leopards and five bears. The Sirkar (Government) gives me Rs. 25 for each tiger and Rs. 5 for each leopard or panther. They don't pay for bears. The villagers also give me four seers (= 9 lbs.) of paddy each, whenever I kill a tiger or panther that has carried off any of their cattle. I also get fed when I am staying at any village. I do all the killing within ten miles of Bara. There are other *bagh-marees* elsewhere.

"We *bagh-marees* chiefly use *dakara* (aconite) for poisoning our arrows. *Dakara* is a root about a span long, and as thick as my wrist. We buy it at Chyebassa from the native medicine shops at four annas a tola. We grind it up with a little boiled rice to make a paste. This paste we rub over a rag, and wind the rag round the back of the arrow-head just behind the barb. The head fits loosely into the shaft of the arrow, so that when the animal is hit the poisoned rag enters the wound with the arrow-head and the shaft drops off. The animal dies within a few hours, and we easily trace it by the blood and broken twigs. Bears are the most difficult to kill. They will sometimes live a whole day with the poisoned arrow inside them. Tigers die very soon. We sometimes use cobra poison, but it is difficult to get. I keep two cobras from which I take the poison once a month. If I take the poison oftener it is of no use. I cannot take the poison while the cobra is changing his skin, which he does once every two months or so. He has no poison then, and won't bite the plantain. How do I get the cobra's poison? Why, I take a ripe plantain and tie it to the end of a stick, and with this I irritate the cobra until he bites the plantain. If he turns his head when he bites, I know the poison has come. He sometimes bites without giving a twist of his head, and then no poison comes. We rub the plantain over the rag, just as we do the *dakara*. A plantain with two bites in it is enough for a large tiger. Cobra poison is the best, as it never spoils; *dakara* gets weaker the longer you keep it. *Dakara* does not grow here; it comes from Calcutta. How do we know where to set our spring bows? *Huzoor*, you know that a tiger never crashes through the brushwood. That would alarm the game. He always takes paths through the jungle. He will not take a narrow path. He sticks his whiskers out straight, and with these he feels the brushwood and knows if there is room for him to pass. He also crouches low when walking. In the dry season there are many paths in the jungle, and as we know not which the tiger will take, we don't usually set our traps in the dry weather. During the rains, when the underwood has grown, we know that the tigers must take the beaten paths, and we set our traps accordingly. The bow is set on V-shaped twigs about eighteen inches from the ground. The bow is placed on one side of the path and a string connected with the trigger stretches across the path, about eighteen inches above the ground, and is tied fast to a twig on the opposite side. If a tiger or panther attempts to follow the path he must breast the string and the strain sets free the poisoned arrows (we generally use two to each bow), which enter his side, and he dies in a few hours within a few hundred yards of the trap. In case men or cattle should stray on to the path, two other strings are attached to the trigger and tied to twigs three and a half feet off the ground and three or four yards away from the trap. This greater height allows a tiger to pass underneath, but should a bullock or a man come that way, he brushes against the higher string, which sets free the arrows before he comes up to them, and they pass harmlessly into the brushwood.

"There is no danger in following up a tiger wounded with poisoned arrows, for even if he is not dead he is so weakened by the potency of the poison that we easily despatch him with our battle-axes. I have never been hurt by a tiger since I was wounded by the witch-panther I told you about. But that was before I became a *bagh-maree*. When we go to a new village we generally make *poojah* (worship), sacrificing a white cock. If we don't make sacrifice we lose our tigers."

This briefly is the story of Beema the *bagh-maree*, elicited from him by a series of questions. The trap used by these native *bagh-marees* is most ingenious and seldom fails; and the danger from them is nil. The weird story of the witch-panther of my friend the *bagh-maree* must be reserved for another occasion.

THE WITCH-PANTHER.

"THE *Huzoor* knows," began my friend the *Bagh-maree*, "that Lagon, the witch, cursed me for asking her for the price of the cloth I made for her. The curse was a great curse and made with bent fingers, and her great toe marked the curse on the sand. After this I was afraid to go to the jungle alone, as I was always in dread of tigers. I killed a cock and sprinkled the blood round my hut, yet the witch's curse was strong and I felt the water on my back the (*Bagh-maree's* definition of fear).

"The *Huzoor* does not believe that our old women can turn themselves into tigers ? But they can do so. All our people know it. It may not be the case with *Sahib-logue* (English people), but with our people it is common. Ask Matha and Lutchman (referring to the village headmen). They will tell you that Lagon can turn herself into any animal she pleases, and do injury to those whom she dislikes. I know that Lagon turned herself into a panther, and killed my goats. I cut at it with my battle-axe, and took off a portion of its ear, and wounded it in the fore-paw. It is well I found and secured the piece of its ear. This saved me, and I knew I was safe so long as I kept this piece in my possession. The next morning, after my goats were killed, Lagon came to my hut and said she heard I had a piece of the tiger's ear, and offered me four rupees for it as she wanted to make medicine with it; but I refused, and then she shut one eye and marked the sand with her big toe and went away. Then I knew it was a question of her life or my life, so I went to Gazee, the Gond, for the charm. Lagon was sick for some time, and did not leave her hut. It was harvest time, and the women were in the fields cutting paddy, and Kunkoo left her baby under the *mahua* tree, within sight of the gleaners. At noon, when the gleaners rested, the baby was gone! Ah, *Huzoor!* the cry that went up when Kunkoo missed her infant! 'Twas the cry of the *chiel* (water-hawk) when its nest is robbed. We searched high, we searched low. The child was too young to crawl, and no one had seen it carried off. Had a *Dave* (goddess) taken it? A few drops of blood leading to the water-course was the first clue. To the water-course we went, and all was plain. The pugs of a panther were plainly seen. Someone remarked that the panther had but three legs, as only three pugs could be traced; the impression of the left fore-paw was missing. We followed the trail to the hills, and there it was lost among the rocks.

"Thereafter scarcely a month passed but we lost some children. The goat-herds were afraid to go to the jungles with their flocks. Not our village alone, but Dalki, Huthutwa, Derwa, and Somij were all haunted by this devil. We knew it to be the same, from the pug marks. It was the three-legged witch-panther. After a time it grew more daring and carried off women. No one would go out alone; while after dark all were afraid, and even the men stayed within their huts. One moonlight night in *Magh* (April-May), when the young men and girls were dancing in the 'house-of-drums' and drinking *mudh* (rice-beer), the witch-panther entered the village and carried off the beer-seller's daughter, a grown young woman of fourteen. No one saw the panther, but the girl was missing and there were the pugs of the three-legged devil. Late next day her feet and a portion of the chest and head were found near Lagon's hut. The old witch was examined, and it was found that she, who had previously been all bones, was now sleek and fat. Some silver ornaments belonging to the *gowla's* daughter, who had been killed by the panther three months before, were found in the witch's hut. The lying old *seeall* (jackal) said she found them while out gathering wood, but we none of us believed her, and it was proposed that we should burn her for having killed our children; but we were afraid of the Sirkar (Government). After taking counsel it was determined that she should be turned out of our village, and her hut burned. This we did that same day, and the *chowkidar* (village watchman) saw her to her relative's house in Morong.

"After this we had no fear, and went about our work as usual, until one day in the rice harvest two years ago. When the paddy is cut we do not thresh it at once, but stack it in piles for a few days, when the ears become loose, and are readily parted from the straw on being trodden by cattle. Our headman and his son and three others were sleeping in the fields near their piles of paddy. In the morning the headman's son was missing, and on search being made, the fatal pugs of the witch-panther were seen. There was weeping in our village, and the most noted *Bagh-marees* were sent for, and traps laid for the witch; but to no purpose. It seemed to be able to avoid all snares. We asked the railway *sahibs* (officials) to come to our help, but although several hunts were organised, and several tigers and panthers killed, yet the dreaded witch-panther still remained at large. When we looked for it in Bara, it was heard of in Derwa, and when we got there, it was back again at Bara. Cocks, goats, and even a buffalo calf were sacrificed, but the panther continued its ravages, and a great fear fell on all the villagers, so that many families left for Patkoom and other places. I alone was not afraid, as I had Gazee's charm, and this kept me safe. Meanwhile the Sirkar offered fifty rupees for the destruction of this brute, but it was of no use.

"Last November, the *Huzoor* will remember, Matho's son, a young man, was taken from his house at night and eaten on the roadway, and only his head and legs were left. The *Huzoor* himself saw this. Then the trap was set at the back of the *bawarchee-khanah* (cook-house), and the witch was killed. At first we did not know it was the witch, but the piece out of the ear proved it was the panther I struck at three years previously, and the broken fore-paw showed it was three-legged. I must have done this also when I cut off its ear. The death of the old woman Lagon about a week after the panther was shot proved conclusively that she was the witch-panther. May her bones be accursed!"

I may here remark that I cannot answer for the truth of all my friend, the *Bagh-maree*, has related of the witch-panther; but on my arrival at Somij I certainly was told of the ravages of a man-eating panther in that neighbourhood. A small panther, about twenty inches high and four feet long (exclusive of tail) was killed with poisoned arrows at the back of my bungalow last November. This, the villagers declare, was the witch-panther. It had only half of one ear, and had lost the use of its left fore-paw. I have the skin to this day.

TREED BY A WILD BUFFALO.

OPINIONS differ as to the best time for buffalo hunting. Some prefer the dry months of March and April. Water, it is argued, is then scarce, and the herds don't stray far from known water-holes. Much depends, I think, on locality. Buffaloes are big feeders and you may have water-holes but no grass, and *then* you are not likely to get buffaloes as they are slow travellers, and will not go long distances away from food to drink. For myself, I like September and October in the forests of Chota Nagpore. Then the rice-fields are one sheet of green, and knee-deep with water from the monsoon rains; and there is nothing these huge brutes like so much as a feed on the young rice and a wallow in the unctuous clay. Indeed, the damage they cause by wallowing in the rice flats is greater than that they do by eating the young shoots of rice, as the natives say that this nibbling off of the top blades makes the rice plant throw out more grain-bearing shoots. In Gangpore, Sarunda and the southern parts of Chota Nagpore, wild buffaloes come down from the hills immediately after the rains set in, and can generally be found near the little patches of rice cultivation dotted here and there in the dense forests of this region. At one time, before the opening of the Bengal-Nagpore Railway, they were very plentiful, and I have known seventeen head fall to a single gun in the course of three weeks. They are rather more difficult to get nowadays, but there are still spots near to the line of railway where you are sure of your buffalo during the *Poojas* (annual native holidays in Bengal, occurring generally in September or October).

As a rule, an Express rifle is almost useless against such a mountain of flesh. Weight of lead tells, and I find a well-planted shot in the neck most effectual, as this is about the most vulnerable part of the *Bubalas arni*. He either drops at once from a broken spinal column, or runs a few hundred yards and falls with a perforated wind-pipe. Some years ago I fired a whole magazine into the shoulders and quarters of a huge bull buffalo before I could get him, and then he only fell from sheer loss of blood. Charun, the famous Kol *shikaree* of Bisra, in Gangpore, put me up to the neck-shot. Charun is a mute, but unlike most mutes he has a very keen sense of hearing, and can detect the stampede of a herd long before the faintest rustle reaches ordinary ears. Although over sixty years of age, he can out-walk the best trackers, and seems never to tire. He was the favourite *shikaree* of Mr. Hewett, a former Chief Commissioner of Chota Nagpore, who presented him with a percussion-cap smooth-bore gun, of which he is very proud. With signs and gestures he easily makes you understand his mean-

8

ing, and I have never known him fail when once on the track of elephant, buffalo or bison.

I was camped near the Bisra station, Bengal-Nagpur Railway, some years ago, when Charun turned up one morning with his arms spread wide over his head—a gesture which I understood to mean buffalo; then a single finger upheld, meaning a solitary buffalo; out-stretched fingers over his foot to indicate the large size of the spoor; adding to the south of the railway line, and that we would come up to it by nine o'clock a.m., by a wave of his hand to the south and pointing to where the sun would be, which conveyed his meaning to me as plainly as words could do. During the rains I find an elephant a very useful animal in a *shikar* expedition. The ground is sloppy; there are numerous rivulets to cross, and after a fatiguing day the return to camp is better done on a pad than on foot. Again, the trophies of the day's sport can easily be brought home if your pad-elephant is kept a few hundred yards behind the trackers. Bheestie, the baggage elephant, was soon in full swing after Charun, who stalked on before, accompanied by two other of his *confrères*, while I was safely perched up on the pad behind the *mahout*. I had only a double 12 smooth-bore—my heavy elephant rifle being away at Calcutta undergoing repair—and Charun had his cap-gun. After crossing some low hills to the south of the line, we turned up a valley to the west, keeping along the course of a *nullah* (dry river-bed) for a mile, when Charun signalled to us to dismount and pointed out the tracks of a buffalo, plainly seen in the soft mud. The foot-prints were of enormous size, fully seven inches from front to rear, indicating that the beast was of the largest size. Instructing the *mahout* to keep within sight, we followed up the trail rapidly. In a small paddy-flat, miles away from any village, we saw where he had had a wallow and had trampled down a large part of the field. Charun signed to us now to be careful as the bull was not far off, and kept throwing quick glances from side to side, as it is a well-known habit of these solitary bulls before resting to make a slight detour and come back to within sight of their own tracks, so as to see any animal that might be following them up. We had just cleared the little paddy-flat and had got into the heavy forest beyond, when we heard a shrill scream from Bheestie, the elephant, and saw her floundering across the flat with apparently another elephant behind her urging her on. Trumpet after trumpet from Bheestie, and the yells of the *mahout* soon made it clear that the second animal was none other than the solitary bull, who had probably made a detour and hidden himself in the dense jungle near his tracks. Why he had allowed us to pass and then charged the elephant it was hard at the time to say, as these brutes will not charge unless wounded or hard pressed; but an explanation was forthcoming afterwards. Anyhow, there he was, prodding at Bheestie behind, and fairly lifting her off her hind legs, while she let out a shrill scream at each successive prod. The soft clay and water of the flat prevented them from making much progress, and gave us time to clamber up a large tree near the side of the flat. The elephant, followed by the buffalo, was making in our direction, and just as they were nearing the edge of the flat I thought I had a good mark at the bull and fired. He stopped for a moment, looked up, and seeing nothing but Bheestie's quarters before him charged furiously into them, and sent her clean out of the flat and on to her shoulder, the pad flying off at the same time. The *mahout* miraculously escaped and ran off to a neighbouring tree. Bheestie soon regained her feet, and went off into the forest trumpeting loudly. After his furious charge the bull apparently slipped and fell on his knees, and while in that position I was able to put in a second shot. There was no doubt about his being hit this time, for over he went on his side; but he was up again in a moment, and charged the elephant-pad which was lying on the margin of the flat. He tossed it high into the air and about ten yards to the front, and it was barely down when he was on to it again, pounding it with his forelegs and dancing on it. I never saw such an exhibition of rage and exultation as that pictured in the mad trampling of the pad by the furious buffalo. He would retreat a few paces, eye the pad a moment, and then rush forward as if to toss it again, but changing his mind at the last moment, would trample it instead. I now had time to put in a third and a fourth shot, but without any marked effect. Charun then let slip his cloth, and waved it up and down. Catching sight of the cloth the bull charged it furiously, and came with such a thud against the trunk of the tree on which we were seated that he made it quiver again, while he himself was thrown quite off his legs by the impact. Charun had now an opportunity, and with my permission, fired. The bull regained his feet and looked about, apparently dazed with the shock of his mad rush against the tree. Charun again waved his cloth, and the bull looking up caught sight of me. Down went his head, up went his tail, and he careered wildly in a circle round the tree, tossing an imaginary enemy at times. He did this several times, stopping at each turn to look up at us, stamp with his feet, emit a bellowing grunt, and then circle round again. The grunt of the wild buffalo is exactly like that of the tiger, and it would require a trained ear to tell the difference at a distance. I feel sure, from the accounts one often hears of tigers roaring at nights, that the noise is frequently only the bellowing of the buffalo or bison. Experienced native *shikarees* tell me that the male tiger seldom roars; while the tigress is noisy only when she is in season.

Covered with mud from head to foot, with masses of soft clay adhering to the long hair on his forehead, the bull looked a strange sight, peering at us with his small eyes, stamping his forelegs impatiently, and bellowing his challenge to us to come down and try conclusions with him. There was no use firing at his head with a smooth-bore, so I tried a shot on the back, meaning to break his spine. Evidently my shot struck one of his ribs, and glanced off, making a deep wound in his stomach, for we saw the blood gushing out as he galloped off some fifty paces, and then turned and watched us from behind a large tree. He had now had six bullets at close range, and yet he appeared full of life. After a time he went down on his fours, and, with his head between his knees, kept watching us. We now began to realise that we were "treed" by the buffalo, and that we might be kept there all day and all night until such time as the beast cared to move off, unless we could make an end of him. There was no use looking for relief from the camp, as there was no one there to relieve us. The elephant might make her way home, but the *mahout* was as much a prisoner as we were, and there was no one to bring her back even if she did return, so we could expect no help from that quarter. There was nothing for it therefore but to sit it out, especially as I had but three more cartridges left, and it would not do to blaze those away and be left defenceless. One of the other trackers thought the buffalo would go for water at about noon, but Charun shook his head, pointing first to the sun and then under his feet, to show that it would be midnight before our foe would give us a chance of escape. Here was a cheerful look-out! To be kept prisoners on a tree till midnight, and it was not yet noon! We must try and draw our enemy and get another chance of a close shot. Charun let down his cloth several times, but the brute had grown too wary and would not move. The men declared they saw his eyes gleam and his head move as he watched us, so none dared to get down. I was beginning to feel the constrained position on the branch, and in an attempt to change it I dropped my gun! Worse and worse. No use attempting to attract the bull now, as we had only Charun's gun and one charge. Natives seldom take out more than a second charge for their guns. We waited an hour, and then Charun signed that he was going down the tree for my gun. I knew that he could swarm up a tree much quicker than I could, so I allowed him to try. He got down very carefully on the side of the tree furthest from the bull, then going on his stomach crawled to the gun, and springing to his feet ran to the tree. His next move took me by surprise. I saw him coolly stalking in the direction of the buffalo. I shouted to him to be careful, but he went on heedless. What had come over the man? Had he become dazed? I expected each moment to see him tossed high in the air by the infuriated monster, and I kept his gun on the cock to try the effects of a shot to stop the charge I momentarily expected. When he got to within ten paces of the bull he stopped, and motioned to us that the beast was dead. We made haste to get down, and found that such was indeed the case. It had been dead an hour or more. In fact, it must have died immediately after it went down on its fours. An arrow sticking in its flank explained the reason why it had charged the elephant when unmolested by us. We learnt afterwards that the Kol who owned the rice-plot had shot it with an arrow shortly before our arrival. It was the pain of this wound that had made the animal furious, and caused it to charge. My last shot in the back had brought about its death, as there was a gaping wound in the stomach from which the blood had flowed in such quantities as to saturate the ground under him. He was certainly the largest bull I had ever shot, and I think one of the largest ever seen in the forests of Chota Nagpore. The elephant was recovered next day and was uninjured; there was not, in fact, a mark of the buffalo's horns on her stern. This was due to the extreme forward curvature of the points of the horns, showing the great age of the buffalo. This adventure did Bheesti a lot of good, for finding she sustained no injury from this close attack she became fearless, and would afterwards stand the charge of a tiger.

THE WILD MAN OF THE WOODS.

PERHAPS there is no profession in the world that brings one more closely into contact with uncivilised man than that of the mining engineer. The nature of his calling—the exploitation of untrodden ground in the search for metals—takes him away from the haunts of civilisation into wilds unutterable, the home of savage man and beast.

In the winter of 1890 I was engaged in prospecting for gold on the hills forming the boundary between the native States of Bonai and Keonjur, in South-Western Bengal. The whole of that portion of the Bengal Presidency known as Chota Nagpore, or more correctly Chutia Nagpur, together with the Tributary Mehals of Orissa, are for the most part made up of hills varying from one to four thousand feet in height, and covered with dense forests of *sâl*, *dhor*, *arsun* and other valuable timber. Until the opening of the Bengal-Nagpore Railway, which now passes through the heart of this region, this part of the country was scarcely known to Europeans. Witch-burning, human sacrifice (*meriah*), and cannibalism were until very recently universally practised by the savage tribes inhabiting this wild region, and the records of the criminal courts at Rañchee and Chyebassa show that instances of these horrible practices are not unknown even at the present day. The tribes inhabiting this tract of country are chiefly of Kolarian descent, supposed by some to be the oldest of the races which invaded India from the North-East; by others, the aborigines of the country.

The particular district I was prospecting is, perhaps, the least known part of this wild region. The hills here rise to over four thousand feet in elevation and are covered with dense vegetation. Few and far between are the small patches of cultivation surrounding the huts of a few Lurka Khols, Bhumijs and Gonds. It is in fact the boast of the Raja of one of these States that he can ride forty miles in a direct line within his dominions without seeing human habitation. Wheeled traffic is unknown on the uplands, and it was with the greatest difficulty that my camp baggage had been transported thus far on pack bullocks. My little hill tent had been pitched on the banks of the Korsua, an affluent of the Brahmini river, in Bonai, and I was working up towards the Keonjur frontier. It was midday. We had done a heavy tramp along the banks of the little stream, washing a dish or two of earth as we went, in all likely-looking places. The yellow metal was scarce, and beyond a "colour or two" our day's work had been blank. I had with me Mookroo, my Khol handy-

NATIVE TRACKERS.

[*To face page* 122.

man, and a couple of Jhora gold-washers. We were resting awhile under the shade of a huge *sâl* tree; my companions were eating a little snuff—a common stimulant among men, women and children in these parts—and I was stretched at full length and munching a biscuit, when suddenly all of us sprang to our feet as peal upon peal of girlish laughter rang out from the direction of a pool of deep water in the river a hundred yards or so below the spot where we were resting.

Who could it be? There was not a village within ten miles. My own camp was fully that distance down stream, yet the laughter was certainly human and girlish. Mookroo was off at once to reconnoitre, while we stood silent and expectant. The Khol returned in a few minutes and told us it was a party of Juangs, or wild people, who had come down to the pool to bathe, and that the women and children were in the water, and probably the men were in the forest on the other side. I had heard much of the Juangs, by some described as gigantic monkeys, by others as wild people of the woods, who wore no clothing and lived in trees. Mookroo asked us to be cautious if we wished to see them, as the least unusual sound would send them off into the forest, like frightened deer. We made a detour and stealthily advanced in the direction of the pool, where a strange sight met our gaze. The whole party, consisting of ten persons, men, women and children, were assembled on the bank, performing their toilet. The women were innocent of clothing beyond the garb of mother Eve after her expulsion from the Garden of Eden, but instead of fig-leaves sewn together, each Juang woman had a narrow cord round the waist to which were suspended a few *sâl* leaves in front, and a large bunch behind. I afterwards learnt that it is only the married women that are permitted by Juang custom to use even such little covering, the unmarried girls going entirely naked. The men wear a narrow strip of the wild plantain bark as a *lungotee*. I asked Mookroo if he could induce them to come over to our side of the stream. "*Hejumay! Hejumay!* (Come here! Come here!)" he shouted in the Khol dialect, and the whole group vanished as if they had sunk into the ground. Not a rustle in the bushes, not a moving object to be seen; yet they were there just now, and gone the instant after. We searched the ground minutely without finding any trace of them. I was much disappointed, as I wished to make a closer acquaintance with this wild people. Mookroo said that if the Jhoras and I would return to camp, he would remain behind, and he felt confident he would be able to induce them to visit my camp if I promised them tobacco, of which they were very fond.

We accordingly set out for camp, leaving the Khol behind. I was having a cup of tea at about five p.m., when Mookroo advanced, and said that the Juangs had come. With some difficulty they were induced to come up to my tent—a grey-headed old man leading the way.

In addition to the grey-head there were two men in their prime, an old woman, three grown women and three children. Apparently the white man was as much an object of curiosity to them as they were to me. A liberal donation of tobacco, rice and coarse sugar soon made us good friends, and they quickly lost all their fear. They spoke a dialect of the Khol language, and through Mookroo I learnt much of their manners and customs. The men were armed with bows and arrows. The bows were made of bamboo, the string also being a thin strip of that material. The arrows were of reed, tipped with a round knob of bamboo, and were most curiously feathered. Instead of three straight lines of feathering, there was a perfect spiral of plumes at the string end, giving the arrow a screw motion when in flight. The blunt knob arrows are used for shooting birds. The men wore strings of beads round the neck and feathers in the hair, and a strip of plantain bark suspended from the waist. The women wore no covering of any kind. Some months later a party of seventeen of these strange folk visited my camp at Somij and asked for work. They would not live in a hut, which they said choked them, but took to the forest and lived under the trees. They generally seek the shelter of a large overhanging rock, and against this they rest a few branches torn from the neighbouring trees, creep within this passage and kindle a fire at the two openings. I found they could do very little work, as they were averse to continued labour.

At mid-day the women would ask leave to go into the forest to change their leaves, which had by that time become crisp and begun to fall to pieces from the heat. After they had been with me a week, I directed my store-keeper to supply each of the women with a few yards of cloth, as I thought it was their poverty alone that prevented their clothing themselves. Next day the whole of them struck work, and the men came to me with a complaint that if their women were compelled to wear clothing, they would all leave, as only bad women wore clothing! Eve's garment was a symbol of innocence with them. Polyandry is practised among these people, or more correctly communism, since the married women are the property of the sept or tribe. They appear to have no notion of numbers except *one* and *many*. They cannot grasp the idea of two. I asked one woman how many children she had. She said, "Many—not one, but many." She had but two. They measure limited time by the withering of the *sâl* leaf. "How far is such a place?" "As far as two *sâl* leaves take to wither," *i.e.*, twelve hours' journey or thirty-six miles, a *sâl* leaf taking, they say, about six hours to wither. Different seasons of the year are determined by such expressions as "When the pea-fowl lay," "when the *mohua* tree blooms," "in the rice harvest," "when the nights are cold."

On one occasion I was treated to a Juang nautch, and certainly nothing quainter or more amusing in the terpsichorean art has come under my notice. The women do all the dancing, the men taking only a subordinate part. They would not dance before my bungalow. I had to go to the forest to witness the dancing. A small clearing of undergrowth had been made in the jungle near my bungalow, and on one side of this clearing the spectators were asked to station themselves. The first item on the programme was the "Peacock Dance." The clearing was quite bare; the Juangs were nowhere to be seen. Suddenly the harsh scream of the peacock was heard some distance off. The imitation was perfect. Now there was a rustling in the bushes, and three Juang maidens, squatting low on their hams, with arms bent close to their sides to represent wings and necks craned forward as if listening, showed themselves on the edge of the clearing. After peering about in the quaintest manner for a few seconds, they all three hopped forward (still on their hams) and began chasing one another about, heads almost touching the ground, and emitting the peculiar chirp of pea-hens when performing their matutinal frolic. Now one would throw up the leaves and earth with her feet, and pretend to pick up food. If another hen attempted to eat in the same place, there was a rush at the poacher, and a few *sâl* leaves were torn from her tail amid shrill screams as she took to flight. Now enters the cock bird, distinguished from the hens by its greater abundance of *sâl* leaves for a tail and a tuft of leaves on the head. With one hand spreading the tail high and giving it a jerky motion, he struts round the females, just as a turkey-cock does. Suddenly he stops his strut, as the scream of a rival is heard in the distance. His tail is at once dropped from its elevated position, his head thrown back and chest protruded. Then the head is shot forward and the answering challenge is given, as he advances in the direction of his expected rival. The scream is repeated several times by the rival cocks, and then the combat begins. This was the most amusing part of the show, and must be seen in its utter ludicrousness to be appreciated. Watch a pair of country cocks making a great show of fight, yet half-afraid to come to close quarters, and you have a good idea of what took place. The two women representing the peacocks would face each other, about ten paces apart, heads lowered to the dust, and their attitude seeming to say, "Come on, if you dare!" Then one would begin to crow, but before he was half through his note of defiance, the other would prance forward a few paces. This went on until they came face to face—and now for the duel! Heads wagging close together, and tails jerking spasmodically, suddenly both birds spin round, and clash come their tails together, and the feathers (leaves) fly. Again they face, and again they spin round, and bang go the tail bunches, amid the shrieks of laughter of the hen birds. Now they spin round continuously, the tails going "whack, whack," till no tails are left, when one of the combatants sinks down exhausted, and with a shrill scream of triumph the victor struts off with the hens.

The vulture dance is even quainter. In the peacock dance only the women take part. In the vulture dance, one of the young men enacts the part of the carcase discovered by the vultures. The carcase is discovered in the centre of the clearing, and one of the vultures (girls squatting, as before, on their hams) hops round it cautiously, stopping now and again to peer at the carrion. Now comes a second vulture, and joins in the hop round. Then a third, a fourth and several others join in the circle, which goes hopping round the carcase, approaching nearer and nearer at each turn. At last one vulture rushes forward and makes a tug at the great toe of the youth representing the dead body. Should he show the faintest symptom of having felt the pinch, he is greeted with shouts of derisive laughter from all the girls, in which the spectators join. If he remains unmoved, the fun goes on, and another vulture rushes forward, and pulls his hair ; a third grips one of his fingers ; then there is a general pinching of his body and much fun and laughing. At last, one bolder than the rest jumps on to the prostrate body, which is too much for the patient youth, who squirms and wriggles as half-a-dozen more jump on to him, and finally he runs off amidst shouts of laughter from all.

There were also a jackal dance and a crocodile dance gone through, but the two dances described were the most amusing.

A WATER-HOOPOO.

READERS of African travel and adventures will remember the descriptions given of the method adopted by the natives in the capture of game on a large scale in Central and South Africa. The scene of the hunt is carefully selected in some locality where game abounds, care being taken that the natural conformation of the ground shall assist in the object of the hunt. A V-shaped stockade is then erected, each leg of which extends perhaps for a mile. The entrance of the stockade is also about a mile wide. Near the apex of the V the stockade is made very strong to resist the attacks of the animals driven into it. At the apex is a small opening, and immediately beyond this an enormous pit is dug, some fifteen feet deep and fifty feet square, with perpendicular sides.

When a beat is arranged the inhabitants of the neighbouring villages assemble, and men, women, and children assist in driving the country for miles towards the entrance of the *hoopoo*, as the trap is called. This may take some days, and is slowly and cautiously conducted, in order to prevent the game becoming alarmed and breaking through the line of beaters. The villagers encamp on the ground and light their fires at night, and gradually advance during the day until all the game in the selected area is within the two sides of the *hoopoo*. Now the women and children retire, and the men, armed with bows, arrows, spears, etc., advance with loud shouts, so that the terrified animals within the stockade rush tumultuously towards the apex only to be engulfed in the yawning pit at the small opening. The animals in front cannot turn back at sight of the pit, as they are pushed on by those behind, and soon the pit is one living mass of game of all kinds, large and small—deer of all kinds, pig, buffalo, rhino, giraffe, lions, panthers and even the lordly elephant. The first in the pit are trampled out of all shape by the succeeding animals tumbling on to them. When the pit is full, what is left of the game within the stockade escapes over the bodies of their comrades. Then ensues a scene of rejoicing and butchering, of cutting up and dividing, till each village has its share of the spoil and the villagers go home with meat enough to last for weeks.

A water *hoopoo* is a hunt after fish, and is arranged in somewhat the same style. I will give a description of such a hunt, which I witnessed recently.

In parts of Western Bengal are a tribe of Gonds known as Jhoras. These people are professional gold-washers and fishers. That is, they are engaged during the rainy months, when water is everywhere available, in washing the sands in the

9*

small streams and rivulets among the hills of Chota Nagpore for the small specks of gold they contain; and during the dry months when the rivers are low they take to fishing. The gold-washing gives them a precarious livelihood; the fishing time is a season of abundance—of feasting, rejoicing and rice-beer drinking. The planning of the water *hoopoo* and the water hunt is directed by the most experienced Jhora present, and as one-sixteenth of the whole catch falls to his share, the post of headman of the hunt is a most lucrative one. My boatman, Samoo, was chosen on this particular occasion, as he had been chosen for the three previous years, and a better choice could not have been made. He seems as perfectly acquainted with the habits of fish as the most experienced *shikaree* is with the habits of the denizens of the jungle. Every nook and cranny, every pool and rapid, all the favourite resorts of the various families of the finny tribe for miles around are known to him. He is as familiar with the reaches of the Koel and Karo rivers for miles above and below their junction, as he is with the inside of his own hut.

The river was low, great stretches of sand and thin streaks of water made up its bed. It was fordable in most places. A deep pool at the junction of the two rivers was selected by Samoo as the terminal of the *hoopoo*. The pool is nearly circular, about one hundred feet in diameter and about sixteen feet deep, with a shelving bank on one side. This was enclosed on three sides by deep nets secured by long bamboo floats at the surface and sinking down to the sand at the bottom. On the fourth side is the shelving bank. All the villagers from the hamlets for miles around had assembled, numbering over three hundred persons. Of these, about forty were fishermen (Jhoras). A stockade of nets closed the passages up and down river, leaving open only one channel which led to the pool. One party of Jhòras went down the river for half a mile and the others up stream, and spreading themselves across the river began beating down towards the pool. In deep water the dug-outs were used, and by constant splashing of the water and striking the surface violently with paddles, the fish were gradually frightened into the pool. At the pool itself all was quiet. Only the headman and myself were allowed near while the driving was going on. Unlike the land *hoopoo*, where the game is silently driven into the stockade and frightened with a rush into the pit, in the water *hoopoo* all the noise was made away from the nets, and the beaters are not allowed to approach within two hundred yards of the pool. Samoo, the headman, was watching the pool intently the while. He seemed to be able to peer down into its very depths. The fish driven from up and down stream, and compelled by the nets to keep to one particular channel which led to the pool, were soon safe within the enclosure. At a signal from Samoo the dug-outs rushed forward and closed the entrance to the pool with nets, and some fifty men plunged into the water and took up positions about six feet from one another outside the nets surrounding the pool. In a moment all was life and animation. Dug-outs and rafts and youngsters on logs of wood suddenly made their appearance and took up places outside the nets. These were gradually worked in towards the landing place. The men would dive down and shift the bottom of the nets a few feet at a time, taking particular care to see that while the net was passing over the rocks at the bottom of the pool, there was no passage left unguarded by the meshes. The Jhoras, by the way, are splendid divers and swimmers. I believe they can keep longer under water than even the amphibious Somali diving boys so familiar to steamship travellers at Aden.

As the space becomes contracted by the gradual approach of the nets, the water within the pool appears to be alive with fish. One particular kind, called locally the *rowee*, leaps clean out of the water for many feet and frequently falls into the canoes and rafts outside the line of nets. The eager rush of the occupants to secure the prize often upsets the frail craft and pitches its freight into the water. But this only excites bursts of laughter from the assembled crowd. On the shore too all is excitement. Men and boys armed with bows and arrows shoot the larger fish as they show at the surface. The head of the arrow is a trident, and to the arrow is attached a long string, which serves to draw in the fish or recover the weapon. When an extra large fish is thus struck, it takes several men and much play before it is landed.

When the nets approach shallow water, several Jhoras enter within the circle of nets and skilfully scooping out the fish with their hands, fling them on to the shore ; here others are ready with battle-axes, and a blow on the head stops all floundering. Fish of from ten to fifteen pounds in weight are thus thrown out and dispatched. A great number also are entangled in the nets, and these are killed with a blow from a club. When it is thought that all the fish over a span long have been secured, the women and children are allowed to enter the water and take what they can get. And now ensues a scene of laughter and mirth. Women armed with baskets, others with portions of their clothes used as nets, others again with pieces of mats, rush pell-mell into the water, shouting and screaming, laughing and tumbling, yet still with an eye to business. Soon the pond is cleared of even its tiniest occupant ; and now begins the division of the spoil.

Immemorial custom has decided that the headman shall get a sixteenth. One-half goes to the Jhoras taking part in the hunt, and one-fourth to the villagers (cultivators and others) present. A sixteenth goes to the owners of the nets and canoes ; another sixteenth to the zemindar—in this case the Takoor of Anandapore ; and the remaining sixteenth is taken by the priests.

It is easy to calculate the catch. I had the curiosity to weigh the share of the headman. This amounted to ninety-two pounds and was made up of forty-four fish, of which three were over ten pounds each, the bulk being under half a pound. The take of large fish over a span long was nearly one thousand five hundred pounds, and perhaps the fifteen baskets of small fish would weigh about five hundred pounds, so that the entire take was two thousand pounds of fish—not a bad day's work for four hundred people.

A brief description of one or two of the more numerous varieties of fish thus caught may not be uninteresting. A large scaleless kind is very like the *becktie* (pike), and at this season of the year was large with roe; some of these were quite three and a half feet long and over ten pounds in weight. The *rowee*, a scaly fish, is very like the *mahseer* in appearance and is very delicate eating. The river herring is about double the size of our Yarmouth favourite, but, unlike that dainty, is only edible around the stomach, though from here a pound of the most delicious eating can be cut. An ugly monster is the *kana*, which looks for all the world like a ground shark in miniature. A spotted hide, tiny eyes, numerous feelers, an enormous head and jaws and powerful tail make the resemblance very close. It lurks among the rocks and seizes any fish that may approach. Its flesh is pink, very like that of salmon.

With the division of spoil the day's labour did not end. A bright moon at night lighted up the scene and showed the sand-bars where the natives were curing the fish over smoky fires. This smoking and a three days' drying over a slow fire keep the fish sweet without the addition of salt. The art of kippering apparently is not a new one. It was known to the Egyptians four thousand years ago; and here we have a wild race perfectly well acquainted with the art of curing without the aid of salt. Their dried fish will keep for years, and the smoky flavour is not at all unpalatable.

A second and a third *hoopoo* were arranged in other parts of the river during the same week, but neither of these was as successful as the first.

THE WHITE TIGER.

"THE Sahib wishes to know which is the most dangerous animal I have ever killed? What do we *baghmarees* (tiger-slayers) know of danger? We set our traps, and it is *nusseeb ka bath* (a question of luck) whether we kill or not. There is no danger. The bow is fixed in the evening, and we go to see next morning whether the arrow is shot. We follow the trail and generally get the animal that day or the next. Bears are the most difficult to kill; not only do they take longer to die, but they generally make off to their caves when wounded and die there. No, we never go near the wounded animal. We follow it up, and if it shows signs of life we go away and come later on, when it is dead. When we use cobra poison the wounded animal goes to sleep and dies in its sleep. *Dakara* (aconite) is also good. *Krait* (snake) poison is not so good. When the arrow has been poisoned with *krait* venom the animal may recover if there be much bleeding from the wound. Yes, we have antidotes for all the poisons. Sometimes a man is wounded by our poisoned arrows. If we know it in time, we apply certain jungle leaves as a poultice and the man recovers. If large water blisters form round the wound within half-an-hour, the man will recover. If no blisters come, he will die.

"What has all this to do with dangerous animals? the Sahib asks. Well, hear me. I was once in great danger. Twenty men were in fear of their lives for a week because of one animal. It was in Gangpore, seven years ago. The Sahib knows the *motee-joad* (twin pearls). Yes, the Sahib has seen it; he shot one on the river a fortnight ago—the large brown-breasted wild duck, that is called by us the *motee-joad* because when once these birds pair their affection for one another is so strong that it has passed into a proverb with us—"As faithful as the *motee-joad*." What affection can be greater? When the *Huzoor* shot the wild duck, its mate would not leave the spot for hours although all its companions had taken to flight, and the *Huzoor* could have shot it also but that his heart is soft. At night these birds do not roost together, but rest on opposite sides of the river, and all night long you will hear their *qua! qua!* as they call to each other. The Sahib is impatient, but I am coming to my story of the white tiger. Yes, *white* tiger. Your servant does not lie. Why should I lie to the Sahib? These eyes have seen it, and others have seen it but they are not here now. White tiger, not panther;—does not your servant know the difference between a tiger and a leopard when he has lived all his life in the forest? Yes, there are white tigers in Gangpore, and I have killed one. It was at the *ghur* (Gainghur, the Raja's residence). A tiger had killed several cattle. The pugs were small and some said it was a panther; but I knew it was a tiger because the pugs of a tiger show the toe marks distinctly, whereas in a panther's pugs the toe marks are very faint, because it treads more on the ball of the foot, to preserve its claws for tree climbing. The tiger cannot climb trees but the panther can. I have seen it run up a tree like a squirrel and bite a man's leg on the topmost bough. On a tree you are safe from a tiger.

"I said it was a tiger, and the Raja asked me to kill it. I set my bow and poisoned arrows near the next kill but the tiger did not come near it. I set it at several different kills but the thief of a tiger was too cunning. He would not come near it. The people laughed and said I was a *tantee* (weaver), and not a *baghmaree* (tiger-killer), and that I had better go back to my trade. But the *Huzoor* can see I am a man"—stroking his moustache—"and am not to be beaten by a *janwar* (wild animal). I took counsel with no one but walked the jungle every day to see if I could not circumvent this dog that had thrown dirt in my face and caused the villagers to laugh at me. I soon noticed that there were two sets of pugs, which went together. This led me to believe there were a tiger and a tigress. I went to every kill before the Khols got scent of it and carried away the flesh, as these people eat every kind of flesh, even rats and snakes and carrion, and I carefully noted that the trails all led in one direction—to a rocky hill covered with dense jungle. This was where the tigers had taken up their abode. I soon found that the tigers took a particular path to the river to drink. That was the clue I wanted. I would now have my revenge, and the villagers would see I was a real *baghmaree*, although only a weaver by caste. *Shabash!* I set my bow to command the path the tiger took when going to the river, and went home quite pleased with myself; but I did not tell anybody that I had set my trap, as I waited for my triumph to be complete. I hardly slept that night, and was away at grey dawn to see the trap. The bow was sprung and both arrows had taken effect as they were not to be found anywhere, while pug marks, blood and signs of struggling were to be seen on the path. I knew the arrows would do their work, for I had put on some fresh cobra poison the previous day. Imagine my feelings, Sahib, when I saw I had triumphed! The bridegroom on his wedding-day, when the village girls anoint him with turmeric and oil; or when you have just secured a pair of strong buffaloes for your plough at half price; or when your field has yielded forty-fold; or when your enemy is dead—mine were all these feelings in one! I felt a hero. I gathered up my bow and ropes and walked to the village a new man. I went straight to the gathering-tree in the centre of the village and sat down. First came one and jibed, 'Well, *tantee* (weaver), is that your loom you have rolled up?' pointing to my bow. 'Make me a *saree* (woman's garment) for my wife, and I will give you half a candy of grain when the crop comes,' said another. Many joined in the laugh, but I waited quietly till the principal men of the village had assembled to talk, when I said, 'Brothers, don't laugh any more, but come with the poor weaver. I have something to show'; and I strode on with the gait of an elephant with the great Maharaj on his back. All the village followed, and I led straight to the place where I had set my trap, and the trail from there was clear. Not two hundred yards off we found the body of the tiger. It was a white tiger. Pure white: no spot or stripe of any kind. Believe me, Sahib, when I tell you it was white. A great shout went up from the villagers and I was happy. Such moments come seldom.

"After a time the villagers left and only the *shikarees* (hunters) of the village remained with me to do *pooja* (religious ceremony). The oldest of the *shikarees* made a slight wound in my head and took some of the blood and rubbed it in on the head of the tiger. I walked three times round the body of the tiger, and then touched its body with my forehead while the others looked aside. We now slung the tiger to a pole and took it to the village in triumph. When we got there, the *shikarees'* wives came out and washed my feet with water and *salaamed* to me. You don't want to hear all that—you want to know where the danger came in. I will pass over the triumphs of the day; how the Raja gave me two rupees and a *dhotee* (cloth); how the villagers also rewarded me, each according to his means. I was a great man that day. Don't be impatient, Sahib; one likes to talk of one's victories—we are all alike.

"We skinned the tiger, and found it was very old—fifteen years old. How do we know a tiger's age? By the number of lobes in the liver. This one had fifteen distinct marks, one for each year. Panthers have these marks also, but not other animals. All *shikarees* know this, as we always take out the liver for medicine. This is how we judge of a tiger's age, and it is true. We pegged out the skin in the sun to dry, the head being boned and stuffed with straw and the mouth agape. At night we rolled up the skin and placed it on some sticks in an empty cow-shed. Our huts were about thirty yards away; but beside the empty shed was another in which several bullocks were stalled. It was barely dark when we heard the 'ough! ough!' of the other tiger in the distance. This we knew was the tiger calling for his mate. The tiger seldom cries, only when calling its mate; it never speaks at other times. Soon the 'ough! ough!' came nearer, and we knew the tiger had scented out his dead mate. Soon it was near the cattle-shed, and we could hear the cattle struggling in alarm. We all shouted together, but the tiger still kept prowling round and round the empty shed. He then sprang on to the roof and tore away the thatch. We now kept very quiet as we began to be afraid. We heard a purring sound and then a roar, and the tiger was inside the empty shed. Soon we heard a great crashing and breaking of wood, and the whole roof of the shed was torn down. He then passed into the next shed, where the bullocks were stalled. The bullocks were so terrified that they broke the barred gate and ran out; but the tiger was down among them and killed four, as we found next morning. He went back to the empty shed and kept alternately roaring and purring. He would go off a couple of hundred yards and roar, and finding no answering roar he would come back. He kept this up the whole night. The whole village was in a fright; not a soul slept. At dawn the tiger went off to the hills, still roaring occasionally. Next morning what a scene met our eyes. Thick bamboos had been bitten in two by the tiger in his rage. The shed was completely wrecked, but the skin was intact. We took the skin to the *ghur* (house) two miles away, where the Raja lived, and told our tale. An old Khol, who knew the habits of all wild beasts, said it was a *motee-joad bagh* (twin-pearl tiger), and that it would never leave its mate, but would kill all in the village unless we killed it. The Raja ordered the skin to be put into a strong shed where the grain was stored, and commanded twenty of the best shooters in the village to get up into *machans* near the shed and shoot the tiger when it came at night. Everybody strongly barricaded their doors that night. I was on a *machan* near the shed. Night came on, but no tiger roared. It grew late; half the night went by; and from fear and trembling we grew light-hearted, and began to twit the Khol about his knowledge of tigers. Suddenly we heard a roar at our very feet that made us lie down and cover our heads in fear. Then we heard a great scratching at the door of the shed where the skin was, and we knew the tiger was trying to break in. We could not see the tiger, so some of us shouted and others fired their guns, but he continued scratching and roaring. We then arranged to fire together at the door in the hopes of hitting him. We fired and heard a scream of rage and then a great scuffling as if something was trying to climb the tree on which our *machan* was built. Of the eight men on my *machan*, six had fired off their matchlocks, and only two shots were left. If the tiger succeeded in climbing the tree we were dead men. I can assure you, Huzoor, I was like a twisted rag; there was no sap in me. The tiger would rush up the trunk of the tree, and then fall back. This he did several times, and then went back to the door and began his scratching. When the other men had reloaded, we arranged to fire four at a time. This we did several times, and at last it appeared as if we had struck him, for the scratching ceased, but he continued to roar. We kept on firing till all sounds from him ceased, and then we knew we had killed him, or he had gone off. In the morning we saw he was dead near the door and near to his mate. He had twenty shots in his body. He was, in truth, a *motee-joad*. He gave up his life rather than leave his mate!"

BEARS AT CLOSE QUARTERS.

"HAS the Sahib got any ball cartridges? There are bears about, and that is better *shikar* (sport) than green pigeon. How do I know that there are bears about? Look yonder; do you see that haze above those trees? It looks like thin smoke; but that is a cloud of flying white ants which are swarming now, after this morning's rain. Do you see those birds flying in and out of the haze? They are feeding on the ants which are issuing in myriads from the ant-hill at the foot of the tree. Those large birds are hornbills, and they would not fly about like that and eat the ants on the wing, if they were not disturbed. They would sit round the ant-hill and pick up the ants as they issue from their holes. There is a bear at that ant-hill eating the ants. It has driven away the birds. All animals are fond of flying white ants. Dogs, jackals, cats, tigers, leopards, bears, birds of all kinds and even men will gorge on them. They are sweeter than new corn and taste like cocoa-nut. Oh, yes; I have eaten them, and if the sahib will only once taste them he will always eat them. Bears like them better even than *mahua* fruit, and I feel sure we shall find a bear under those trees, if the sahib will come."

Luckily I had with me a couple of ball cartridges, so I told the Purdhan, or headman of Dalki, who was out with me shooting green pigeon, to lead the way. A few hundred yards up the steep slope of the hill and under the shade of lofty forest-trees, a strange scene presented itself. Crows, minas, jays, the great and little hornbill, swallows, finches, and birds of all kinds were darting hither and thither amid great chattering and cawing, after white-ants which were taking the wing in thousands. At the foot of a decayed tree, near to which was an ant-hill, a female bear and two well-grown cubs were literally licking up the flying-ants as they issued from their holes. Slobbering their forepaws over with saliva, they brought them down on the ants, whose thin gauze-like wings adhered to the wet paws, and were thus easily licked off by the bears. So busy were they at this evidently delectable occupation, and so intent on securing as much as possible of this dainty, that we were able to approach unobserved to within fifty yards. The wary crows alone spotted us and flew off a little way, but soon returned to the feast. A perfect cloud of ants went up like a haze from the foot of the tree, and into this flying mass the birds darted open-mouthed, greedily gobbling up the toothsome morsels. The shrill notes of the smaller birds, the hoarse caw of the crows, and the harsh scream of the hornbills made such a noise that it was possible to approach much nearer without being heard. I stood gazing at this strange scene for fully five minutes, when suddenly I heard a shot some twenty yards in advance of me, and then found that the Purdhan had stolen away unobserved by me and had had a pot at the bears on his own account. All was still in a moment. The birds flew off on the report of the gun, and the cubs also bolted; but I could see that the she-bear was struck in the side, as she bit viciously at the wounded part, growling savagely as she tugged out bunches of hair. The Purdhan now attempted to retreat to where I was concealed, and in his flitting from tree to tree the bear caught sight of him and at once gave chase. It is astonishing the pace such a clumsy-looking animal as Bruin can put on. Before the man got half-way to me the bear nearly overtook him, and it was only by dodging behind the trunk of a large tree that he escaped her clutches. Finding the man had stopped, she rose on her hind legs and with her snout elevated high in the air gave vent to a series of short snapping howls, such as one hears from the tame animals brought round by showmen when irritated. With a kind of a waddle she advanced to the tree and clutched at the trunk, but it was much too thick for her to get at her foe. Down she now went on her fours and chivied the man round and round, but here he had the advantage, as he could turn more quickly than the bear and so kept well out of her reach. After a dozen turns or more, finding she could not reach him, she once more rose on her hind legs and began clawing the trunk of the tree and scoring the bark with her great nails. Then she stuffed both forepaws into her mouth and began biting them, grunting savagely the whole time.

The Purdhan shouted to me to shoot, but the whole scene looked so ridiculous and there seemed to be so little immediate danger that I decided to await developments. Finding no satisfaction apparently in biting her own paws, down she went again and after the headman as hard as she could go. Anon she would rise on her hind legs and hop forward in the most comical manner, and then down again. How long this would have lasted it is hard to tell, as natives are long-winded and can keep up a race for miles; but now an unforeseen danger threatened, which made me regret that I had not fired before. The cubs, which had bolted on the report of the first shot, finding their dam did not follow them and probably hearing her growling, now came shambling up. Although not quite full-grown, they were large enough to make formidable opponents to an unarmed man, and it would be all up with the headman if they came to the assistance of their mother. Only two ball cartridges left and three bears to face! A bear robbed of her whelps has passed into a proverb for ferocity, but a wounded bear with her cubs present is even worse. There was not much time for deliberation. Shouting to the Purdhan to throw his turban at the she-bear and then run towards me, I decided to let her have both barrels when she stopped to worry the turban, and to take our chance with the cubs. As I anticipated, she at once clutched at the turban and began tearing it to shreds, while the Purdhan flew towards me. Aiming low, as she was at close range and the shots might rise in their trajectory, I fired both barrels in rapid succession. Over she went a regular somersault and kept turning over and over every time she attempted to rise. Presently she got on to three legs and began staggering along after her cubs, which had again bolted on the noise of the firing. It was evident that the bone of one of her forelegs was broken, as the paw hung limp by her side. Now and again she would stop and look back at us, as if not quite decided whether she would return to the attack or not. The Purdhan was for bolting, but I threatened to knock him down if he attempted to move, as I knew that to run away would be a direct invitation to the bear to attack, and with only No. 6 shot in my gun a bear, even though badly wounded, would make short work of us. We could hear her savage growls as she went shambling up the hillside to her cave in the rocks above. Next morning, with a better provided magazine, we followed up her trail, and found she had taken refuge in a cave on the hill-top. We could distinctly hear the gurgling sound that bears make when sucking their paws—a sound closely resembling that of a hubble-bubble (native hookah) when smoked—but all our endeavours to get them to break cover were fruitless. Stones, firebrands, repeated shots—all were ineffectual, and I had to return empty-handed, resolving mentally never again to go bear-shooting when after green pigeon.

MY SHIKAREE FRIENDS.—III.

PURDASEE, THE DOM.

My first acquaintance with Purdasee was under circumstances of so terrible a character that I can never forget them. It was during the dreadful famine of 1877–78, when upwards of five million persons died from starvation and disease engendered from a scarcity of food in South India. Out of a population of five and a quarter millions, Mysore lost a million and a quarter, while the Bellary district suffered even more severely. In Madras mountains of grain in bags were stacked all along the sea-shore, brought in by ships from Calcutta, Burmah, Gopalpore and elsewhere, but transport into the interior—to the districts most affected by the famine—was utterly inadequate. The Madras Railway in those days terminated at Bangalore on the south-west and at Bellary on the north-west, while the whole of the large stretch of country between these two towns was entirely without railways. Cattle had suffered even more severely than human beings during these two seasons of drought, so that even transport in bullock-carts was sadly crippled.

In parts of the Bellary district and in North Mysore grain there was none, and whole villages were depopulated, the inhabitants literally dying of starvation. I was through the worst parts of these two districts during this terrible time, and the awful sights of mute human suffering that met my gaze I have no wish to recall.

To come to my story. I was riding along the high road between Chitaldroog and Bellary a few days before Christmas, and was anxious to make the latter town in order to get in to Bangalore by Christmas day. I had ridden across country some twenty miles and had just struck the high-road and hoped to fall in with my camp, which I had sent on a few days in advance, to await me at a large village I had named. The country through which I had ridden was extremely desolate. At that time of the year the fields should have been laden with *cholum* (millet), which thrives wonderfully on the black cotton soil of Bellary; but the failure of the North-east monsoon had resulted in a very scanty crop, which was plucked and eaten by the starving population before it had even had time to ripen. I had gone about a couple of miles when I noticed a few huts a hundred yards off the road, and as I was anxious to hear of my baggage I rode over to see if the villagers could tell me whether my carts had gone on. I shouted when I came to the huts, but no one answered. Some of the huts were closed, others open, but there did not seem to be a soul about. I was just about to ride off when I heard some low moans near a thicket of milk-hedge (euphorbia). On going to the spot I was witness of a most horrible sight. A couple of village *pariah* dogs were tugging at the legs of a man, trying to drag him out of a small hut of millet stalks. The poor wretch was so emaciated and weak from starvation that he had not the strength to beat them off, but was clinging convulsively to the sides of the hut and moaning faintly now and again. A shower of blows with my whip failed to drive off the dogs, which had grown ferocious by feeding on human corpses, so that I had to draw my revolver and shoot one of them before the other took to flight. My terrible experiences of the previous few months had taught me that the village dogs, grown savage with hunger, had taken to feeding on the bodies of the dead and dying villagers, and had I not opportunely arrived when I did, they would have made short work of the poor wretch in the hut. My syce now came up, and I sent him on to hunt up my camp and to bring some villagers with a *charpoy* (village bedstead) on which to carry the poor fellow to my tent. A few drops of brandy from my flask soon revived him, and he greedily devoured a biscuit moistened in brandy. I could see that hunger was his chief ailment, but I would not for the present give him more than a second biscuit, as I knew that in extreme cases such as his, food must be administered with caution. After a little time he was able to sit up, and he then told me he did not belong to the village, but was one of a party of Doms or Pahariahs (hill-men), who were on their way to the wooded tracts to the South-east. They had been without food for days, and on the bare plain in this part of the country there were no birds to snare. They found the village deserted, and as he was too weak to follow his people they had left him in the hut to die. He had lain there all the previous day, and not a soul had come near the village. At night the dogs had smelt him out and attempted to attack him, but he had beaten them off. They renewed their attack in the morning and he again kept them off, but only for a time, as they had recommenced their attack and would certainly have killed him had I not come up and saved him from being eaten by them. "Ough!" the poor wretch quivered and fainted off.

In a little time my *chuprassee* (messenger) came up with several villagers and a *charpoy*, and the poor fellow was carried to my camp and taken care of by my servants.

On my return to camp after the Christmas vacation I found Purdasee much better. Purdasee was not his real name, but on being asked who he was, he said he was a "Purdasee" (literally a man from foreign parts, but used colloquially to designate anyone extremely poor); so the name stuck to him. He belonged to the great clan of wanderers and outcasts found all over India and known under various names, such as Doms, Ghassias, Bhujs, Kooravers, etc. They are wanderers all of them, having no settled habitation,

IN CAMP, ON A SHOOTING TRIP.

[*To face page* 154.

but with a few donkeys to carry their household pots and baggage may be seen on the outskirts of most Indian villages. The women weave mats and tell fortunes; while the men snare birds and lift hen-roosts. They are notorious thieves, and not a fowl, kid, or cat is safe for miles round their encampment. Of the flesh of the cat these people are particularly fond, and when later on I occasionally took Purdasee with me into Bangalore many a fine Tabby mysteriously disappeared, to the surprise and grief of its owner. It was no use expostulating with Purdasee. His sense of *meum* and *tuum* was dead as regards tabbies. His gratitude to me for saving his life was heartfelt, but I really believe that even that would have counted for little if weighed in the balance against his love for cat's flesh.

It took several months before Purdasee thoroughly recovered his strength and was able to accompany my camp. He then attached himself to my tent, would assist in pitching it, and would hang around all day for some word or notice from me. In the wooded districts he proved a great aid to my commissariat, as never a day passed but he brought in quail, partridge, pea-fowl, jungle cock, etc. He was expert at all kinds of snares, traps, nets, nooses and devices for trapping birds and small animals. He was also a most perfect mimic and could imitate the cry of the jackal, partridge, quail and jungle fowl. I have several times been present when he has decoyed birds, hare and jackal into his traps, and I could not for the life of me tell the difference between his call and that of the animals he imitated. Was it jackal he wanted—he would partly shade his mouth with his left hand and a series of yells would break forth, as if all the jackals had assembled to join chorus. He could make the notes sound distant or near by merely opening and closing his hand. If he were after a quail, the "ronk" of the male bird was heard to perfection. From the thigh bones of a cat he shaped a whistle from which the strangest sounds would issue at will. Far off larks would come down in flight, or crow-pheasants and pea-fowl would answer the harsh scream. Sometimes he would be absent for days, and then he would return with a low flat basket filled with partridges and quail on his head, a long rod slung across his shoulder and a peacock perched on either side. To prevent the pea-fowl taking to flight he would sew their eyelids together with a small feather, so that they could not see, and in that condition they remained perfectly quiet on their perch and could be handled.

Purdasee was delighted when work took me to the wooded districts. There he was in his element, snaring game. On the plains he could only exercise his ingenuity on the village roosters, and when he found that I compelled him to take them back to their owners, and that he was in disfavour for the remainder of the day, he brought me no more village fowl; but I felt sure that the thieving went on all the same, as he would find ready receivers in my camp servants, who were not so scrupulous as to how the fowls were come by. I asked him one day how he managed to catch the fowls without noise. He said he drugged them with rice which he kept in his mouth all night. It fermented there and became very intoxicating. The fowls eating this rice became drunk and stupid, and were easily caught.

Poor Purdasee! He fell a victim to his devotion to me. I was out fowling one day and had shot a couple of duck in a tank (pond), but found that they were too far out and the water too deep to recover them by wading. I sent Purdasee to see if he could find a villager who could swim, but all of them said they could not. I turned away disappointed, and was wending my way home when a villager ran up and said that Purdasee had gone into the tank after the duck and had not returned. We instituted a most careful search, and constructing a couple of rafts, I had the tank carefully dragged in the direction where he was last seen, but without result. His body was not recovered till two days later. Poor Purdasee!

HUNTING WILD DOGS IN A DUG-OUT.

"*Sahib, Sahib, bagh! Nudhee may—do bagh!*" (Sir, Sir, a tiger in the river—two tigers!)

It was early dawn—perhaps five o'clock—and the cool morning breeze in July induced sleep after a restless night passed in the muggy warm atmosphere of the monsoon. However, the *khubber* (news) of two tigers under my very nose sent sleep to the winds, and I was up in a moment and hastened out in my slippers to get full particulars from my "kit" (valet) who was standing expectant at the doorway. The villagers had reported that two tigers were swimming over the river towards my bungalow, which was situated on the right bank of the Koel river. The tigers were said to be now in mid-stream, and the villagers were assembled on the bank and shouting to keep them off. A most hideous yell, or rather succession of yells, heard at that moment proved that the latter part at least of the "kit's" story was true. No time to dress, so seizing four ball cartridges for my double-barrelled 12-bore, I hastened down to the river.

The recent heavy rains had raised the water-level twenty feet and the Koel was full from bank to bank, a seething, swirling volume of yellow liquid, dotted all over with floating masses of foam. The river at this point is about 200 yards wide in mid-stream, and some 300 yards further up two black objects could be plainly seen among the masses of foam, breasting the current and swimming vigorously up stream.

The flood had prevented the ferrying over of some score of carts on their way to Beru, so that on the left bank were assembled all the carters and their following. On the right bank were the villagers of Somij, armed with bows, spears and matchlocks. These two crowds lining the banks kept the animals —whatever they were—from landing. A dug-out was speedily launched, and two sturdy Jhoras (fishermen) armed with paddles took their places at bow and stern. For the information of the uninitiated I may say that a dug-out is a tree log of light wood, some twenty feet long and fifteen inches in diameter. The ends are pointed like the bows and stern of a canoe, and the trunk hollowed out. To trust one's self in such an unstable craft, even in still waters, requires a good deal of nerve, as it is impossible to stand upright without danger of overbalancing this primitive contrivance; but to face it in a rough, boisterous stream in flood required the excitement of the chase after a brace of tigers to enable one to screw up one's courage to the sticking point and venture forth.

The dug-out speeded on its way, propelled by

two pairs of strong arms, but once we were in mid-current it required all the efforts of the boatmen to stem the raging stream and make headway. The two "tigers" were now some 350 yards up stream, and it really seemed wonderful how these animals could make headway in such a mill-race. Finding we could make little progress in mid-stream, I directed the canoe-men to get nearer the bank into slack water, and when we were abreast of the animals to shoot out again into the centre. When we got within fifty yards we perceived that the so-called "tigers" were nothing more than a pair of wild dogs. So great was my disappointment that I was inclined to direct the boatmen to return, but I suppose that the innate love of bloodshed said to be characteristic of man prevailed, and we continued the chase. The wild-dogs now perceived our approach, and putting on a spurt actually distanced the dug-out, although with alternate promises of reward and punishment I urged the Jhoras to do their utmost. Finding their efforts unavailing I fired at the nearest dog, which was about fifty yards ahead. I missed—the mark being a very bad one, as I dared not stand and all that I could see of the brute was its ears and nose; however, the shot was sufficient to turn its fellow, which now made down stream, still keeping to the centre. It passed within twenty yards of me, but I could not fire for fear of the bullet glancing off the water and hitting one of the many people who lined the bank. I therefore directed the boatmen to turn and follow this one, as I made quite sure we could come up with it going down stream. By the time we had turned it had got forty yards' start of us, and it kept that distance for nearly half a mile. I never saw such swimming in all my life. It was simply racing speed. We must have been going eight miles an hour (the current being four and a half to five), and yet we had not gained ten yards in that half-mile race! The excitement was intense, the crowds shouting and running along the banks, while I was using very unparliamentary language to urge the boatmen on, and the poor brute doing its best to get away. The river Karo joins the Koel on its left bank, about half a mile below my bungalow, and as the cartmen on the left bank could not cross the Karo, the animal would find the bank free, if it managed to clear the Karo. The creature saw this at a glance, and put forth all its efforts to gain this point. We in the dug-out also saw that if not overtaken before it crossed the junction of the rivers it would escape. Now then for the final struggle. The dug-out seemed to fly through the water, yet the dog kept its distance and crossed the Karo. In making for the shore however it got into slack water, and here we gained perceptibly. A last chance offered when the animal got within ten yards of the long grass edging the river. I fired and again missed, and the dog disappeared in the dense undergrowth. I must say that I was scarcely sorry I had missed. The chase had lasted nearly an hour, up stream and down, and the animal had beaten the boat in both directions. Its exertions were truly marvellous, and I would not have believed any land animal capable of such powers of swimming had I not witnessed this wild-dog's efforts to escape.

We now turned our attention to its fellow, which we saw some two hundred yards up stream, following in the direction its mate had taken. The dugout was hastily drawn under some overhanging branches, and we silently awaited the approach of the animal. When within ten yards a shot smashed his skull, and he sank to rise again some distance down stream. The boatmen neatly harpooned him, and brought him to land. He proved to be a full-grown male, of a reddish-brown colour, flecked with a little black about the face and ears. The tail ended in a tuft of hair. In size he was very much larger than the wild-dogs of Southern India and more nearly resembled the dingo of South Australia. Marvellous were the tales the villagers related of the prowess of the wild-dog. According to native accounts a pack of wild dogs when pressed by hunger will not hesitate to attack a tiger.

A MAD ELEPHANT.

"HONORED SIR,—I would bring to your honor's kind recollection the caprices of a demented mad elephant, and ask for your honor's instructions in the same. He is beastly bad one, and notwithstanding that he has already suicided thirty-three of his defunct relatives, he now is murderously intent on all having a similitude to his kind, in the appearance of domestic milch buffaloes; and thereafter. He has raided all the villages in the environs of No. 2 Division, and the coolies and ryots are frightened for the lives and persons, although he has not yet crimed the man-slaughter, but only the buffaloes and not the cows. Mr. Theobald is here just now, and wants your honor's geenerous advice to shoot or otherwise this furious packshidedams. The fire-lines are awaiting the monster's removal, as the men wont work, in fear and trembling. A quick response will ever be grateful to your most humble servant,

"S. RAMALINGUM,

"Sp. Ranger, F. A., Madras University.

"To the Assistant Forest Officer,
"Kollegal Division, Coimbatore."

The above is a true copy of a letter addressed to the Assistant Conservator of Forests a few years ago by one of the native subordinates of the Forest Department, and gives in native B.A. English a graphic account of the doings of a mad elephant then at large in the forests of Kollegal, bordering the Mysore Province. The history of this brute is well worth relating, as his madness took a very singular form, his fury seeming to be directed against his own kind or anything bearing a resemblance thereto.

Complaints had for some time been pouring in to the Collector of Coimbatore of the destruction to fields of corn and sugar-cane by herds of wild elephants which came down from the hills in Kollegal, and laid waste the cultivation in the low country. As it would be dfficult to shoot down whole herds of these animals it was determined to build a *kheddah*, or elephant trap, capture the brutes wholesale, and break them in to forest work as beasts of burden. A series of stockades and enclosures were accordingly constructed in the bottom of a densely wooded valley draining into the river Cauvery. Hundreds of beaters had been assembled and a herd of thirty-three huge animals had been successfully driven into the impounding stockade, and the heavy gate of logs made fast. Watchmen had been told off to feed great fires surrounding the stockade and to prevent all attempts of the captured herd to break through the log-fence and ditch of the *kheddah*. There was much jubilation throughout the camp. The Collector was there with numerous guests who had come down from Ootacamund and neighbouring stations to witness the drive. Next day was to be devoted to separating the wild herd and to hobbling individual elephants and making them fast to trees, as a preliminary to

A BABY ELEPHANT.

[*To face page* 164.

breaking them in. The aid of half-a-dozen *koonkies*, or female elephants specially trained to assist in the dangerous operation of securing and making fast their wild brethren, had been obtained, and several large tuskers were also present to overawe any of the captured ones that might show fight. All was quiet for the night. The guests had retired to their tents after a late dinner; the tame elephants had gone to their camp some half-a-mile away; the watchmen were dozing over their watch-fires—when suddenly a fierce trumpeting was heard from within the *kheddah*, followed by a squealing and shrieking as if a legion of pigs were being slaughtered. The din was terrific; the whole herd seemed to have gone mad. There was a rushing here and a rushing there, as the huge animals tumbled over one another in their fright. By the light of the moon and the blaze of the watch-fires, now heaped with faggots, a perfect mountain of flesh could be seen huddled up in one corner of the *kheddah*—elephant over elephant, a writhing mass which heaved and squealed and groaned in the vain efforts of those undermost to escape from the vast overburden of their fellows, who came tumbling on the top of them in the attempt to escape from some object of terror behind. The shouts of the watchers, the din of tom-toms (drums), the bray of trumpets and the springing of rattles added to the noise and confusion. The camp was now thoroughly alarmed but no one could tell what had happened. That there was something very wrong within the *kheddah* was evident, but what it was none could say. Most of those assembled at the camp had climbed into trees overlooking the *kheddah*, and could see the huge black masses huddled on one another and squealing most shrilly. Now and again there would be an interval of silence within the *kheddah* and the mountain of flesh would disentangle itself and the elephants hurry off here and there, leaving many of their number dead or dying. The tame elephants were sent for and soon arrived on the scene, but none dared to enter the enclosure, so appalling was the sight that gradually unfolded itself. The whole enclosure was strewed with dead and dying elephants, and a huge tusker was seen driving deep his tusks into the bodies of his fallen victims, stamping on those that showed the least signs of life, and kicking the carcases here and there in his diabolical rage, emitting at the same time the most unearthly yells and screams that had ever been heard from one of these brutes. When satisfied that the body before him was lifeless, away he would charge after the herd and single out another victim. There was no escape. The enclosure was of limited extent, and strewn as it was with the bodies of dead and dying elephants it prevented any lengthened chase. Elephant after elephant had fallen before his blind fury, and now all was still within. By this time the spectators of this ghastly scene had formed some idea of what had happened, and the guns were sent for. None of the tame elephants would approach the *kheddah*. They appeared to know what had happened, and with trunk elevated they scented the air, and knew there was danger for themselves if they approached the raving brute. The trees were too far off to permit of a good shot at him from among the branches, and the only place that appeared at all likely to give a chance was at the great drop gate. T——, taking one of the oldest native *shikaris* with him, made for this point of vantage and waited patiently the approach of the mad elephant, which was going round the enclosure turning over the bodies of those it had killed and stamping out what remained of life in those that had escaped his first furious onset. Aiming as best he could, T—— fired, and shouted to the *shikari* to escape through a narrow postern in the palisading making the avenue which led to the gate, as he saw that his shot had failed and the raging brute was charging down on them. The native seemed paralysed with terror, or believed in the strength of the gate, and would not move. T—— barely escaped through the opening, when crash went the strong timbers of the gate like matchwood before the terrible impact. The white clothing of the *shikari* caught the elephant's eye. In a moment his trunk was round the unfortunate man, and placing a foot on one leg and seizing the other in its trunk it simply tore the poor wretch in two and threw the pieces high into the air. With a demoniac trumpet it then charged down the avenue, and was away to the hills before the horrified spectators could fairly grasp what had occurred.

The morning showed a dreadful sight within the *kheddah*. The earth, sodden with the blood of the elephants, had been churned into a quagmire by their ponderous feet in their wild rushes to escape from their mad companion. Great bodies strewed the enclosure, some mangled and trodden out of all semblance to the living creature. In one corner the bodies were so piled up and mixed together that it was difficult to conceive how they could have got into that position. This mass showed some movement, and with immense difficulty two living elephants were exhumed from this veritable mountain of flesh. All the others were dead. Of the thirty-three leviathans captured the previous evening, thirty dead bodies, two maimed brutes more than half-dead, and the runaway made up the tale!

Great heavens! Could this scene of slaughter be the work of one brute! Was it possible for one animal to destroy thirty of his fellows in the space of a couple of hours? Many of the victims were as large as, if not larger than, their mad assailant, and two were immense tuskers. The labour of six months and a large expenditure of money gone in an hour! The herd when secured would have been worth more than half a lakh of rupees (Rs. 50,000), now all gone through the instrumentality of one luckless brute; and, more than this, one ill-fated human being had been torn limb from limb.

Nothing more was heard of the runaway for some time. Then came in reports from numerous villages bordering the forest lands of Kollegal of the depredations of a mad elephant. His insanity took a peculiar form, as I have said, inasmuch as it was directed against his own kind and against buffaloes. He killed two of the forest elephants engaged in timber work, so that the working elephants had to be removed. He would enter a village, make for the cattle enclosures and destroy every buffalo he saw. Bullocks he would not touch, nor did he show any particular animosity to human beings; but buffaloes seemed to be his pet aversion. On one occasion he kept a whole village within their huts for two days in his vain attempts to enter a stone enclosure, such as the natives use for penning cattle, in which there was a herd of buffaloes.

A large Government reward was now offered for his destruction, and numerous native *shikarees* endeavoured to bag him without success. He was frequently shot at and received many wounds, and at length became so wary that he was seldom seen, and it was only news of his continued depredations—here to-day, twenty miles off next day—that kept up the terror of his name.

The story of how this cunning brute was circumvented and at length laid low I will tell in another chapter.

THE FATE OF THE *AHNAY PAYEE*.

So numerous were the petitions to the Collector of Coimbatore regarding the damage done by the mad elephant—of which some account was given in the last chapter—that special means had to be devised to rid the district of its presence. Not only had it killed thirty of the herd captured in the *kheddah*, but since that night's savage work it had destroyed half-a-dozen more tame elephants, belonging to Government and private individuals. Buffaloes by the score had also fallen victims to its peculiar form of insanity, and so great was the terror it inspired that many villages on the Kollegal frontier were abandoned, with the result that cultivation suffered and forest work was much impeded. Mr. Theobald, the well-known assistant to Mr. Sanderson, the elephant-catcher, at that time a Forest Officer in the employ of the Madras Government and known to be a keen *shikaree*, was deputed on special duty to endeavour to shoot the brute. It had now been at large for about six months and during that time it had done an immense amount of damage. Traps of all kinds—pitfalls, spring-guns, balanced spears, nooses, decoys

—all had been tried, but without effect. It had been wounded several times and had now become so wary that it lay concealed during the day and made its attacks only on the darkest nights. It was so cunning that immediately after destroying the buffaloes in a village it would leave that locality at once, and be next heard of twenty or thirty miles away. Another peculiarity about it was that it never travelled the same path twice, as if it were aware that danger was most likely to be met along those tracks. The Government reward for its destruction was high, so that many native *shikarees* from the neighbouring districts had been attracted to Kollegal in hopes of securing it; but all their efforts had proved fruitless. The elephant was seldom seen; yet the damage went on all the same. The Tamil inhabitants of the district called it the *Ahnay Payee* (elephant devil), and offered sacrifices of cocks and sheep to appease its wrath. Captain Godfrey, the famous elephant-killer from the Wynaad, spent a month in search of the brute but never once caught sight of it. Such was the animal Theobald was now directed to destroy.

His first measures were to collect all the native *shikarees* of note and find out from them what had been done and what plans were left untried. As the beast showed such a strong antipathy to buffaloes, it was thought it might be got at by the hunters being concealed in a cattle-pen among buffaloes. An open kraal was accordingly selected, and a pit sunk in the centre. This was protected by a light fencing to keep out the cattle. The hunters spent over a week in this unsavoury spot amid the intolerable smell of the buffaloes and plagued by myriads of insects. On the last night of this vigil, towards midnight, the buffaloes manifested signs of uneasiness. They thronged close up against the side of the kraal furthest from that in which the wind was blowing and, with faces turned windward, seemed to scent something unusual. The night was pitchy dark so that it was impossible to see anything beyond a dozen paces. Now the cattle came rushing to the centre of the kraal and against the light fencing, as if to seek the protection of their human fellows. It appeared as if an opportunity was at last going to offer and the hunters were all alert; but no! the excitement passed off and after a time the cattle returned to their usual positions of repose. The morning showed the tracks of the elephant clearly all round the kraal, but it had not made the slightest attempt to break in. It must have scented its human foes, and made off noiselessly. It was seen therefore that this plan would not answer, so something fresh had to be devised. There was not the slightest use attempting to track the brute for it appeared to be ever on the move, and so cunning had it become that when feeding it would make a dêtour and take up a position from which it could see its own tracks; its hearing and scent also were so acute that it generally detected its pursuers before they saw it, and while they were plodding their way straight ahead, a loud trumpet, as if of derision, on their right or left would show them they were discovered, and it would be twenty miles off in a few hours.

After much cogitation a plan suggested by one of the *mahouts* that looked promising was tried. Two of the most intelligent female elephants employed in forest work were selected, and these were taught to elevate their trunks on the approach of another elephant. The one which first gave warning was always rewarded with some little dainty, so that in a short time they became so clever that another elephant could not approach within several hundred yards but they would scent it out and give warning by elevating their trunks. When sufficiently trained, Theobald mounted on one of these animals, and with two good *shikarees* on the other set out on the trail of the mad elephant. Some fifteen miles of country were traversed on the first day, yet nothing was seen of the runaway. On the second day about noon, while going through some bamboo-covered bottom, both elephants gave sign towards the right of the trail. All was excitement now. The guns were got ready, and with an interval of about four hundred yards between them the tame elephants were moved off to the right and a cautious advance was made. Now was heard a crackle of branches ahead. The brute was probably feeding! The jungle became denser. There, behind a clump, a dark object was seen! Now a gleam of white—his tusks! Yes, a solitary elephant, and a tusker!

It must be the rogue! A still further advance was made, and yet it had not taken the alarm. Another twenty yards and it would be near enough for a shot. Squeal! Squeal! What is that? A baby elephant! And now its mother shows itself, and then another and another. Pshaw! Not the rogue after all! Merely a herd of wild elephants. Another such disappointment and this plan had also to be given up. Theobald was at his wits' end. There was no getting a shot at the wary brute. He now bethought him of some of his Sholiga friends. The Sholigas are a wild race inhabiting the Belligherry Rungan Hills on the Kollegal frontier, and are the most expert trackers of wild beasts in the world, besides being better acquainted with the habits of elephants than any other people. Boomay Gowda, a Sholiga headman (and the expert tracker referred to in the chapter headed "At the Kheddahs"), was under obligation to Theobald. The latter therefore decided to send for him and ask his advice. Boomay Gowda arrived.

"I will bring the mad elephant to the *doray* (gentleman)," he said when he had heard the whole story.

"Bring the mad elephant to me, Boomay Gowda! What? Are you mad yourself?"

"The *doray* will see. Give me a week's time, and I will make the *Ahnay Payee* come up to your place of concealment, so that you can shoot him."

The old man would give no further information.

He would explain matters after the kill, he said. The native *shikarees* and *mahouts* present were inclined to laugh at Boomay Gowda as a *junglee* (a term of contempt among natives, meaning a man from the jungles), but Theobald knew him better. A few days later a Sholiga came to Theobald and said he had been directed by Boomay Gowda to take the hunters to a place of concealment in a water-course some ten miles off, and that they were to camp there till Boomay Gowda arrived. The spot indicated was a dry nullah with a steep rocky bed and banks of clay about ten feet high. The width of the water-course was not more than ten to fifteen feet. Heavy forest trees with little or no underwood covered the country on both banks for miles, so that it was easy to see any object approaching the water-course without oneself being seen. The hunters were directed to camp about a mile away from the water-course on the left bank, and were instructed that when Boomay Gowda came they were to take up a position in the nullah so that their heads would be level with the right bank, from which direction the mad elephant would approach. They were not to climb into a tree or *machan*, as from that height their scent would be wafted far and wide and the elephant would not come; but they were to lie low in the water-course, whence their scent would not be carried to the elephant and they could shoot him as he approached.

Two days afterwards Boomay Gowda came early in the morning and said the elephant would be at the water-course about ten o'clock and that they must hurry off. Theobald and one *shikari* took up a position pointed out to them by the Sholiga in the nullah commanding the right bank. He told them to be careful and not show them·selves nor to make any noise, but to peer over the edge of the bank now and again to see the elephant approach, while he would be off to see that all was right. Perching themselves on a small ledge in the bank they waited till about half-past nine when they saw a huge elephant approaching cautiously from a direction at right angles to the nullah. There was the great brute with the point of his trunk nearly touching the ground, smelling carefully at a trail of some kind. Now and again he would stop and elevate his trunk, turning it on all sides to scent out anything strange. Being reassured, he would again move cautiously forward, still carefully scenting the ground and making direct for the spot where the hunters lay concealed. There all was in readiness. No mistake this time. It was the mad elephant. Theobald would have liked a side-shot just behind the opening of the ear, as he had bagged dozens of elephants each with a single shot there; but from the direction in which the elephant was approaching, there was no chance of the ear-shot, so he determined to take the next best place—the fleshy protuberance in the middle of the forehead. The elephant was advancing slowly, with head lowered, and was now about twenty paces off. Suddenly he stopped and raised his head, with the flaps of his great ears thrown forward. The movement disconcerted Theobald, who fired just as the brute stopped. The shot struck six inches too low, in the hollow where the bones of the head are thickest. There was no time for a second shot. With a scream of rage the elephant was on them, and over them, his tusks embedded deep in the opposite bank. Apparently he had not noticed the nullah in his wild charge, or he could not stop himself if he had seen it.

Theobald and his *shikaree* were knocked off the ledge by great masses of earth hurled from the top of the bank, which gave way under the enormous weight of the charging elephant. In the clouds of dust raised by the falling earth and the struggles of the elephant they managed to scramble to their legs and run up the nullah, without thought of their guns, which fell from their hands when they were knocked over by the clods of earth. The instinct of self-preservation was strong within them, and they knew their lives were not worth a minute's purchase once the elephant got on to his legs. Up stream they scrambled as best they could, over the boulders and loose stones, looking round nervously for a place up which they could clamber out of the nullah; but none offered. They had barely got fifty paces, when they heard a heavy fall of earth, and knew that the elephant had brought down the bank in which its tusks were embedded and was again on its feet. It appeared dazed for the moment, and then looked round in search of its foes. The noise of their running soon attracted it, and with a shrill scream of rage, it was after them. What occurred next is best told in Theobald's own words:

"My legs appeared to give way—I felt as if I could not run another pace. The *shikaree* shot ahead of me, and gained a point some twenty yards in front, where a bush overhung the nullah. With a leap he gained the branches, and was on the bank in safety. Already I thought I felt the cold, clammy clutch of the elephant's trunk round my neck. I was choking! I thought of the poor *shikaree* torn in two at the *kheddah*, and knew that would be my fate in another minute or two, unless I gained the bush up which the *shikaree* had clambered. My legs appeared to be made of lead; I could not for the life of me do more than a trot. '*Iyo! Iyo! hodoo! hodoo cheekrum!*' (O! O! run! run fast!), shouted the *shikaree* from the bank. No! my head began to swim. I could not go faster, when suddenly down the bank leaped Boomay Gowda, and, seizing me by the hand, hurried me along. How we gained the bush, and how we got up the bank, I know not. When I recovered recollection I was standing on the bank, supported by the *shikaree* and Boomay Gowda, while the elephant was below us, trumpetting and screaming as it tore into shreds the bush up which we had escaped, and on which it was now venting its rage. That would have been my fate, I thought, as I squeezed the hand of the brave old man who had just risked his own life for me. Finding it could not get at us, the elephant set off up stream. Were we to lose it after all? Our guns were in the nullah, some hundred yards away. No! here comes a Sholiga with them. Boomay Gowda had sent him off at once for them, immediately we were in safety. 'Come, sir! come this way! The nullah takes a bend up stream, and we can get ahead of the elephant easily,' said Boomay Gowda, and off we set at a run. We got to the bank, and concealed ourselves behind some bushes. Now we heard the elephant coming along, stumbling over the stones, and making as much noise as a whole herd of cattle rushing down a steep. I could see the blood oozing out of the wound in its head, and its face was one mass of blood, with the flicking of its ears. I was quite cool now. It is opposite me, not ten paces off. Its ear is quite exposed. I fire! It drops like a shot. Not a move. Thank God! it is ours!"

Old elephant hunters will recognise at once the plan adopted by Boomay Gowda to bring the elephant to the hunters. It is a device practised by the wild tribes of the Garo Hills, as well as the jungle races in the South of India, to entice male elephants to their pit-falls. Certain ingredients are mixed with water, and this is dropped on the ground, here and there, in the direction in which the male is to be enticed.

HIS FIRST BISON.

"God forgive you, Ned, but I think you have brought me on this tramp purposely, in order to pay me out for the slating I gave you last field-day, when you made such a mess of it. Great Scott! you did get your company mixed up. Could not have done worse if you'd tried. Bison, indeed! and only three miles off! Why, we have been on the tramp since *chota hazree* (early breakfast), and that's four hours ago. The trail is warm? Is it?; not as warm as I am, I can tell you, and I don't budge a foot until I have had a peg; so, banghy-wallah, *baito* (rest) you here, my man, and let us lighten your load. They are just over that ridge, are they? Well, it won't harm them to wait a bit till this child has quenched his thirst. I vote we lunch now, and take them after. You see, if you once get into the heat of the chase we don't know when we may stop. No, no, let us start afresh, I say, as I mean to have a bison this day, and no mistake. Come along, man, sit down; tiffin (lunch)—then bisin—good that, eh?

"Heigho! After tiffin rest awhile. Sound advice that, whoever was the author. He does not say how long; but that, I fancy, should be according to the time of year and the latitude. Here, in Chota Nagpore, and in April, it means till you feel an inclination to move, and that feeling has not come over me yet. Don't be impatient, old chap. One would fancy you are to shoot the bison, and not I. Remember, this is my first bison, and I am all excitement. Catch your hare? Gad, the fellow is becoming sententious. Just see me dance—no, see me on the war-path, and you won't talk of catching. That bison is as good as nobbled. I wonder if W—— will let me put the head up at the head-quarters armoury. Not a bad idea that, a kind of incentive to good shooting among the B. N. R. (Bengal-Nagpur Railway) Volunteers, as each and every man might do likewise. Don't laugh, man; they laugh best who laugh last! Come, I don't mind going you a fiver that the honour and glory of this shoot falls to me.

"Nay, nay, if thou lovest me, Ned, let me rest awhile, and I'll forgive you your next 'spoof' at company drill. This weather is too killing, so be off and kill that bison, for I don't budge till sundown."

Kartik, the *shikaree*, had just returned with *khubber* (news) that the herd was grazing in a glade beyond the ridge, only a mile off. There was no time to lose, so leaving our worthy Adjutant under the shade of the *sâl* tree, I moved off double quick. A smart tramp up the rise, and there was the herd, not six hundred yards off. With my glass I could make out four cows, a couple of well-grown calves, all huddled up together; and in all his lordly majesty, a little distance away from his family, a magnificent bull, keeping watch and ward. This is the usual habit with bison; the master of the herd grazes by himself some little distance away from the rest.

There was a little rough ground to the windward, and I saw that, if I gained that spot there would be the chance of a shot at the big bull, so going down on our stomachs we crawled along as fast as we could, taking advantage of every bit of cover. There is no part of the hunt—not even when you have plugged your beast and brought him down—that equals in excitement the ten minutes or so that elapses between the time when you sight your quarry and the getting within range. Heat, fatigue, wounded hands and knees, all are forgotten! Every moment you expect him to be off. You clutch your gun convulsively as you reach each little scrap of cover, and think "Shall I fire? Is he too far off—another yard or so?" This is the experience of even those who have shot their score and more. It appeared to take only five minutes to crawl the five hundred yards and bring us within range. I was pouring with perspiration, and my eyes were so wet that I could barely see the sights as I got on to my knees and grasped my Paradox. An attempt to brush the moisture from my eyes attracted the attention of one of the cows, and a short warning grunt gave notice to the herd that something unusual was approaching. Instantly every head was turned in our direction. Kartik was much too good a *shikaree* to move. He was flat on his stomach. Any sudden movement on my part would have sent the herd off helter-skelter. Inch by inch I rose to my feet, the whole herd gazing intently at this novel object. Inch by inch, and my Paradox is raised to my shoulder. With an impatient stamp the bull comes a yard or two nearer to view this strange intruder. Ah! the excitement, the intense pleasure of that moment, to know that one clutch of the fingers, and that great brute would be at my feet. Black as jet, with brown to the knees, and a patch of brown on the forehead, he looked superb as, pawing the dust, he gazed in my direction with lowered head ready for the attack. What chance had the heaviest weapon against that massive frontal bone? No, I must not move. I must wait till a vulnerable point offers. Will he never move? At last he raises his head, and sniffs the air, as if to scent out the danger. Fatal movement! He exposes his chest, and a single bullet lays him low, while the remainder of the herd scamper off helter-skelter. I stood with gun at shoulder, ready for a second shot, should he rise and charge, or attempt to make off. The well-trained Kartik was still prone on his stomach, as he knew that, if he moved and attracted the bull's attention, and it had still life enough left to charge, he would be the objective.

A convulsive kick or two, and all was still. Nineteen hands high of flesh and bone had succumbed to an ounce and a half of lead. Five feet seven and a half inches gave the circuit of his horns from tip to tip. He was in his prime, not a bit aged, and in splendid condition.

Kartik was sent off to collect the villagers to bring in the spoil, while I tried the soothing influence of a cigar. Not the slightest fatigue did I feel. The excitement and triumph had carried that off, and I felt fit for another ten-mile tramp. Skilful hands were soon engaged disembowelling him, and even after this, it was as much as thirty men could do to get him on to a *sugger* (village cart) and take him on to the station, as I wished personally to superintend the flaying.

"Well, Ned! drawn a blank?" said the Adjutant. "Thought so. Knew you would spoil matters with your hurry. Now, if you had waited a bit till I was ready, we should have had something to show for all our trouble. Didn't think you would sling a bison at your waist, like a brace of snipe? No, old boy. 'Tis your gills I look at. No triumph there. White, man! white! Gory is the colour of success. Never mind, Ned; take a peg, old man, it will cheer you up. But all said and done, old man, it is a beastly shame your spoiling our day's sport with your impatience. It is just the way with you fellows who know nothing of game and their ways."

Quietly imbibing my peg, I told him the tale

A RECORD BISON.

[*To face page* 184.

of the shoot, every detail being fresh in memory, and success adding an eloquence to my tongue which at other times could barely tell a story of twenty lines coherently.

"Here, *puckerow juldee!* Pack up *ek-dum!* (take hold quick, pack up at once). Gad, we must get into the station sharp, and see that those fellows don't maul our skin. Say, won't we have the laugh of those fellows at C——? We did the trick nicely, didn't we? I feel as if I could do another bull. But I am always in luck. Fellows always like to go out with me; I never draw a blank. Nineteen hands? By Jove, won't the Colonel feel small? He never shot one more than sixteen; and here, at my first attempt, we bag a nineteen-hander. Do you know, I don't feel a bit fatigued. I am as fit as possible."

Two months later, while dining at Nagpore, I heard a full and detailed account of how our Adjutant had bagged his first bison!

THE MONKEY-EATERS.

WHILE tramping along the banks of the northern Karo river, just above the point where it precipitates itself over a waterfall eighty feet high, into the Koel river, in the south-east corner of Lohardugga, in Chota Nagpore, strange shouts of "*hill-hillo-lowee! hill-hillo-lowee! hill-hillo-lowee!*" (with a long pause on the second word) were heard from an elbow in the river a little way up stream. On inquiry I was told that the shouts came from a party of *Behurs*, or monkey-eaters, who were engaged in hunting monkeys, and that if we concealed ourselves and approached cautiously we should be able to witness the hunt, but that the advance must be made carefully, as the *Behurs* are a very wild race who live only in the forests, on the trees, or in holes in the rocks; that they hold no intercourse with any but their own people, and avoid all villages, and that if they saw us they would most likely make off. As the hunt was evidently being made towards the river from its right bank, we went over to the opposite side and concealed ourselves in the forest just opposite the elbow or bend in the river towards which the hunt seemed to be directed. The river, not being more than fifty yards wide at this point, we could distinctly see all that was taking place on the other side. The loud "Whoop! Whoop!" of the *lungur* monkey (a note that can be heard miles off), with the occasional harsh, coughing cry of the animal when alarmed, was now heard in the point of land opposite. The "hill-hillo-ing" approached nearer and nearer, and now we could see the tree tops opposite shaken by the monkeys as they leaped from branch to branch. Presently about a dozen long-tailed, black-faced monkeys appeared in the trees overlooking the river. They would peer down into the water, and then jabber among themselves as if holding a consultation. Several large fellows now descended the trees and approached the stream, in search of a place where to cross. The stream was deep at this point, and much too wide to leap over; and as there is nothing this class of monkey dreads so much as deep water, they made up their minds there was no crossing there. This was soon communicated to their fellows on the trees, and now began a scene of rushing from branch to branch, with shrill screams of fear as the hunters began to draw near them. Several of the *Behurs* were up in the trees armed with bows and arrows, more were on the ground with slings from which they hurled stones into the topmost boughs to drive forth any of the monkeys that might have concealed themselves there. The women and children, armed with sticks and branches, kept on beating the bushes, and shouting "*hill-hillo-lowee! hill-hillo-lowee!*" As they approached, the monkeys, now mad with fear, threw themselves tumultuously from the trees, and scampered off along the sandy margin of the stream, the hunters in hot pursuit. The monkeys were kept to the stream by a line of *Behurs*, who now appeared on the margin, and thus chased, they rushed headlong into nets previously stretched across the sandy shore from the water to the bank, and for some distance along the edge. Into this *cul-de-sac* they were driven, and while entangled in the nets clubbed to death by the *Behurs*. There was not the slightest attempt on their part to show fight, although some of the *lungurs* were of the largest size—quite four feet without the tail—and had large powerful teeth. That *lungurs* can fight I have occasion to remember, in the loss of two fine dogs and the serious injury of another. But now a great fear seemed to come over them, and, huddled up in the nets, they tried to hide themselves under one another as they were mercilessly brained by the clubs of the *Behurs*.

We thought it time to show ourselves, as there was less chance of the hunters running away now that they had bagged their game. Perhaps it was their numbers gave them courage—there were about thirty in all, men, women, and children—and we were but three. The women and children collected the nets, while the men proceeded to flay the monkeys, of which there were a dozen, or more. The skinning was most effectually done in a very simple manner. A small hole was made in the skin of one of the legs. Into this the thumb was inserted, and the flesh separated from the skin for a little distance. A reed was now inserted into the hole, and strongly blown through, so as to inflate the space made by the thumb. The hole was now firmly pinched so as to allow none of the air to escape, and the air squeezed forward with the hands, so that a further portion of the skin was separated from the flesh. This space was now inflated, and the squeezing forward process of the air again carried out, and continued until in a little time the skin was swelled out like a balloon and loosened entirely from the carcase. A hole was now made under the neck, and the whole body withdrawn, or rather the skin was turned back on itself, and pulled off like a sock. The hands were then cut off at the wrist and, the tail being removed at the stump, the skin is rubbed over with powdered wild turmeric, to preserve it from insects. The tails, with skins on, are carefully preserved, and when dried make formidable clubs, quite four feet long and immensely strong; and these are used by the *Behurs* for killing monkeys and other game. The skins find a ready sale among the Gassis and makers of tom-toms (drums), as monkey-skins make better drum-heads than the skin of any other animal.

We found that the Behurs spoke a dialect of Mundaree, or Kol, language common to all the aborigines of Chota Nagpore. A few cigars distributed amongst the men and a handful of coppers among the women and children soon placed them at their ease, and they were ready to answer our questions. For some little time we watched them cutting up the carcases. The liver, heart, and other tit-bits were first removed, and cut up into small pieces and skewered on little sticks and put out in the sun to dry. A certain portion of flesh was put aside for present consumption, and the remainder cut into narrow strips, and hung on a frame-work of green branches under which a fire was kindled and plentifully heaped with green *sâl* leaves, the smoke from which, they said, preserved the meat, so that it would keep for months. It never went bad. In reply to questions put by me, one of the men replied: "Why should we live in houses when we have the forest trees? They shelter us from sun and rain, and give us food; what more do we want? In the rains we have roots of all kinds; in the dry weather we have wild fruit and the larvæ of the red ant, which is good to eat, as it makes us strong. Then there are monkeys and wild pigs, and sometimes a deer. No, we never want; the jungle people never starve; the forest is a beautiful mother. We never live in huts; we sleep under a tree in fine weather, or within the shelter of a rock when it rains. We never go far from the streams, as there is no forest where there is no water. From Surguja to Bonai, from Mohurbhunj to Palamow, we wander along the river banks, and we are content. We go to the *hât* (markets) only for tobacco and salt and to sell our skins."

On being asked, one or two of the men readily showed us how they hunted monkeys. If the animals could be got into a broken portion of forest, they could be readily captured, as they could be driven from one side into the open ground, where the nets were set. Monkeys always ran away from their pursuers, and never tried to break back. If the forest was continuous there was no use hunting them, as they escaped from tree to tree. If the *Behurs* hunted them from the ground they might escape in the branches over their heads, but a certain number of their men were always sent up into the trees, which they climbed almost as expertly as the monkeys themselves. The nets are about four feet wide, and of various lengths, and not much stronger than the ordinary fishing-nets. From the intestines of the monkeys they also make a fine gut, which they manufacture into nooses for snaring pea-fowl, jungle-fowl, partridge, etc.

Their method of catching jungle-fowl is very ingenious. Several tame cocks form part of their stock-in-trade. The early morning is the time chosen for the snaring. A tame cock is fastened by a string attached to its leg to a peg driven in the ground, in the part of the forest selected. Round this is described a complete circle, ten or twelve yards in diameter, the circumference being represented by a thin cord about a foot from the ground, and securely fastened to pegs driven in at intervals. From this cord are hung a number of nooses of monkey gut, so as to enclose the decoy cock in the centre with a circle of snares. The *Behur* now conceals himself in some brushwood near at hand. The tame cock begins to crow, and very soon an answering challenge is heard from some of the jungle cocks. The decoy continues his note of defiance, and presently a jungle-cock is seen in the branches overhead ready to do battle with this intruder on his own peculiar domains. Down he flies towards his opponent, who with ruffled feathers is ready to meet him, and just as they are about to begin battle, the man appears on the scene. This at once frightens off the jungle-cock, which, instead of taking to flight, bends its head low and runs off, and, meeting with the nooses, is almost certain to be caught by the neck or legs. The man quickly bags it, re-adjusts his snares, and goes back to his place of concealment, and the challenge and crowing go on again till all the cocks in the neighbourhood are secured. Four or five birds, sometimes, are secured in this way in the course of a morning.

AFTER A WOUNDED TIGER.

A TIGER having killed a cow at noon, within a couple of hundred yards of my bungalow, the occurrence was promptly reported to me. As I was suffering from fever at the time, I did not care to sit up at night over the kill, so I told the village *baghmaree* (tiger-killer) to set his poisoned arrows. A slight obstruction of branches was made on two sides of the carcase of the cow, the other two sides being left free, so that the tiger might approach to feed. Two bows, each provided with two poisoned arrows, were set to command these paths. On going to the spot next morning we found that the tiger had been there during the night, and had stumbled over the cord attached to the trigger of one of the bows, and that two of the arrows had evidently lodged in its body, as they were not to be found on the spot. Apparently when struck the beast must have sprung forward, and to one side, right on to the other bow, as that had been set off also, the arrows being found a little distance away. The marks of the tiger's pugs and a little hair and blood were strewed about the trap. The natives declared it was sure to be dead in the forest, and they set out in search of it. They came to my bungalow after an hour's time, and said they had found the tiger in a water-course about six hundred yards off, and that it was not dead, but had charged them. I advised them to leave it alone, as a wounded tiger was a very dangerous customer, and I added that they would probably find it dead in the evening, by which time the poisoned arrows would have taken effect.

They came back at four in the afternoon, and told me the tiger was still in the same place, and that it appeared to be very weak, and they asked me to come and shoot it. I did not like to refuse this request as it would appear to the men that I was afraid to go where they had already been. I knew the extreme danger of following up a wounded tiger, yet I could see the natives did not appreciate its full extent, and any further delay on my part would have been put down to fear. In dealing with wild races it is very necessary that you should show them that you are at least as courageous as themselves; if not, they soon lose all respect for you. I told them therefore that I did not care to risk their lives, as they were only armed with battle-axes, but if they promised to remain at my bungalow, I would go, with one of their number to show me the way, and try to shoot the tiger. At first they demurred to letting the *sahib* go alone where there was danger, but finding I was firm, they squatted down near my bungalow, while one man accompanied me. The brute, I found, was last seen in some thick brushwood in the forest, about six hundred yards from my camp. I had with me a double twelve-bore gun and four cartridges. We cautiously approached within twenty yards of the spot where the animal was said to be lying, and sheltering myself behind a large tree, I got my guide to throw stones from behind me into the dense jungle in front. A dozen stones or more had been thrown at the spot where he was last seen and on each side of it, and I was just about to step out from my place of shelter, when I heard a voice behind me exclaim: "Throw the stone further; the tiger is beyond the *mohua* tree." Turning round I saw the whole group of villagers assembled some forty yards off watching me. On remonstrating with them for breaking their word and following me, they remarked, "There is no danger where the *sahib* is; the tiger might have found us alone at the bungalow, and then what should we have done?" As there was thus no help for it, I allowed them to accompany me. They appeared to know no fear, and several times tried to go on in advance of me, but I would not permit them. We carefully searched about, and saw a few drops of blood in places, but no signs of the tiger. As it was now getting dusk I persuaded the men to give up the search, and promised to go out with them the following morning. That night I had a sharp attack of fever, and was up all night. Towards midnight I heard the hideous cry of the "Pheeall," an animal of the jackal kind, which is said to accompany tigers and leopards in their nightly prowls, and to make its supper off their leavings. This night it seemed to me that the "Pheeall's" cry ended off with a plaintive yell, and it kept up this cry for more than an hour, just round the spot where the tiger was said to be lying. My *chuprassee* said this was a sure sign that the tiger was dead, as the "Pheeall" was bemoaning the loss of its supper-finder.

Feeling sure the tiger was dead, I next morning told my *jemadar* (headman) to accompany the men in their search, and gave him my gun with a couple of rounds of ball cartridge, just to lend confidence to the party. The searchers were barely gone half-an-hour when I heard two reports in rapid succession. Fearing some accident, I hastily placed four ball cartridges in my pocket, and ran to the spot where we had searched the previous evening. There I found about a dozen men up in the trees, and my *jemadar* and two villagers coolly searching in the jungle. On inquiry, my *jemadar* told me the tiger was still alive, and had apparently been sleeping all night under some bushes a few paces behind the tree that had sheltered me the previous day; so that while we had been looking for it in front, it was all the time watching us from behind. The wonder is that it did not rush out and attack us! There was its form distinct enough, on the ground, and a little dried blood from the arrow wound. The natives said the tiger was weak from the effect of the poison of the arrows. These arrows had been dipped in *dakara* (aconite) some months previously, and the poison was not strong enough to kill the tiger. My *jemadar* had seen the tiger from some ten or twelve paces off, and had fired, but the first shot missed. The tiger was then bolting, and he fired a second time, and hit it (we found afterwards that this shot struck it in the stomach near the arrow wound). He pointed to fresh drops of blood on the grass, and said he was following these up to find the spot where the tiger had taken shelter, and then he meant to come and tell me. He held the empty gun in his hand, and two other natives had battle-axes with them; yet here they were following up the trail of a wounded tiger! These people really seemed to know no fear. Owing partly to the fever, I myself was a little excited, and taking possession of the gun, and carefully loading and full-cocking it, I directed the men to get behind me while I took up the search myself. The blood marks were faint and the jungle very dense, so I had soon to allow the men to approach and track for me. The whole party was now at my heels assisting in the search. We had gone about two hundred yards or so, the underwood becoming denser every step, and the men had spread out a little, when suddenly, just in front of me, I heard "crunk! crunk! crunk!" and there, only ten paces ahead, and directly facing me, was the tiger, with its mouth agape and emitting the peculiar rasping sound of this animal when irritated. I levelled my gun at its open mouth, and was just about to fire when it sank down behind the bushes out of sight. Keeping my piece still levelled at the spot, I directed the men to retire; but there was no need for this, as all but two had vanished at the first sound of the tiger's note. The names of these two brave men ought to be recorded in print, and I give them here—Lalloo the Tantee, and Purdan the Boomij. These two brave fellows stuck to me and one of them whispered: "Don't fire, sahib, till you see its head, for if you don't kill it with your shot it will kill all three of us." There we stood for a good five minutes peering about, but unable to catch a glimpse of it, so well had it concealed itself, although now and again it would emit a growl and the peculiar gurgling sound tigers make. I now directed Purdan to climb a tree close by and endeavour to see the tiger. This he did, and told me the tiger was still behind the bushes, watching me and lashing its tail. Peer as I would, I could not catch a glimpse of it, and knew it would be foolhardy to advance any nearer. There was a little open ground behind the tiger, and Purdan advised that I should make a *détour* and get a shot from behind, while he remained on the tree. This I proceeded to do, accompanied by Lalloo. The *jemadar* now put in an appearance, and I directed him to get on to a tree also. We had barely been gone five minutes when Purdan shouted that the tiger was making in our direction. There it was, true enough, some fifty yards off, slouching along, and stopping now and again to look in my direction. Directing Lalloo to get behind me I awaited its approach, hoping to get a fair shot at twenty paces distant. When still thirty paces off down it dropped again, and concealed itself. I was once or twice tempted to fire at what I thought was its head among the bushes, but wisely resisted the inclination. My *jemadar* now called to me that he could plainly see the tiger from his perch, and asked me to come round to his side. When I got there he said the tiger was still in the same place, but I could not see it. I endeavoured to climb the tree, but found my efforts unavailing. The *jemadar* said that if I would hand him the gun he was sure he could shoot the brute, as he could see its head plainly. I directed him to fire only one shot, and not on any account to fire the second unless the tiger charged. Handing him my gun, I sheltered myself behind the tree, my heart going pit-a-pat at a furious rate. The *jemadar* now said the tiger had turned and was approaching us; should he fire? —"Yes, fire, but aim at his head."—Bang! "Ough!" roared the tiger, and all was still again. I hastily took the gun and reloaded. We waited a little, and the *jemadar* said the tiger was dead, as it had turned on its back. After a little time we approached, and found the tiger stone dead, the *jemadar's* last shot having struck it fairly over the right eye. We took it home in triumph, and there carefully measured it. It was a tigress, eight feet three inches from nose to tip of tail, and three feet six inches high.

The poisoned arrow had made a nasty wound in the stomach, the arrow-head being still within the wound. It must have been the potency of the poison which had induced the lethargic feeling in the tiger and prevented its charging; otherwise that day might have had a very different ending!

IN CROCODILE VALLEY.

THE finest shooting grounds I know of in India—and I have been over the greater part of the country—are in the Native State of Bonai, in Chota Nagpore. Before the opening of the Bengal-Nagpore Railway, few Europeans ever visited this out-of-the-way district, and even now not a dozen persons know of its existence outside the pages of the Gazetteer. Fifteen hundred square miles of densely-wooded, well-watered hill and dale, never trodden by civilised man, and little troubled with cultivation of any kind, is just the ideal home for wild beasts in India. Within twenty-four hours by railway from Calcutta, the wonder is that it has not been more shot over. Here the lordly elephant, the shaggy bison, the sullen buffalo, the stately sambhur, tigers and their kind, deer of sorts, bears, immense crocodile, wild hogs, pea-fowl, and a dozen other game birds can be had galore. The Raja, a fine old sportsman himself, is only too ready to give permission to European gentlemen to shoot over his estate, and will, on occasion, join in the sport and bring with him a most unique armoury of offensive weapons. He will at such times be attended by match-lock men armed with bell-mouthed smooth-bores, having a barrel seven feet long, and a straight stock with a crutch-end to fit round the shoulder. It takes three men to fire off such a piece. A forked stick is first planted in the ground, and on this the barrel rests. One man places the crutch-end against his shoulder and aims, while a second plants himself immediately behind, back to back, as a buttress against the recoil. A third stands on one side and blows vigorously at the match, and the first brings it down into the pan by means of a rude kind of trigger. The animal is supposed to stand still while all these varied operations are going on! Then there is a fizz-fizz-fizz—bang! And after the volumes of smoke have cleared away, the two men behind the barrel, who have been sent sprawling by the recoil, pick themselves up, carefully search for the gun, which will be lying somewhere about, and then set out to see the effects of the shot. If by chance an animal has been shot, great is the jubilation. The aimer at once takes rank among the Raja's following as a marksman. "If a *janwar* (wild animal) is shot by one of my men it seldom survives," said the Raja; and I can well believe this, for two large handfuls of locally manufactured powder and several murderous-looking slugs form the usual charge of one of these match-locks. Since the opening of the railway the fine *sâl* forests of the valley and the supposed mineral wealth of the State have been the means of increasing the Raja's armoury with specimens of most kinds of modern small arms. Revolvers, rim and central fire; smooth bores; rifles;

Colt's repeating rifles; Paradox and other guns, with and without ammunition, are among the offerings of would-be concessionaires. But our Rajpoot Chief dislikes modern fire-arms, and in this view he is strongly supported by his following. "In modern times everything is getting miserly," says this sturdy representative of the kingly class. "In my time everything was large; men were large, the guns were large, the charges were large, and sport was sport. Now a *puttass* (cracker) goes 'pitt'; there is no noise, no smoke, even the man behind holding the gun is not thrown down; is it likely, then, that the animal in front will be killed? No, no; give me my father's guns, and I am satisfied." Accordingly the well-meant presents of the gun-makers' best work are stored away with time-pieces and cuckoo clocks, tinsel robes of state, mirrors, and other frippery, only to be brought out on State occasions to parade before the Raja's few European visitors. An attempt was once made to utilise some of the ammunition, and on one occasion several central-fire revolver cartridges were rammed into a match-lock as slugs. When discharged the barrel burst, and the man blowing the match had his ear and the greater portion of his scalp taken off, since when even these "modern slugs" are viewed with suspicion.

Bonai is a veritable sportsman's paradise. Are you fond of fishing? The Brahmini river, which flows through the State from north to south, teems with fish of all kinds. Is it a tusker you want? With the Raja's permission you can shoot over the elephant reserves of Jorda and Champa, and take your choice of the herds. Buffalo and bison are plentiful in the deep valleys, and deer everywhere. Quite recently a railway man in a fortnight's time bagged two bison, three buffalo, and several fine *sambhur* in this neighbourhood; while a young gunner shot a tusker whose ivory sold for more than the cost of the trip several times over.

Mountains over four thousand feet high make up the bulk of the State, and through this barrier the Brahmini has cut for itself a passage, making deep valleys on either side. Some idea of the depth of these valleys may be formed when it is stated that Bonai town, on the banks of the river, is only five hundred feet above sea-level, while only nine miles off you are on the top of a range four thousand six hundred feet above the sea; so that it is quite possible to swelter in the heat of the valleys in March during the day, and get back at night to the bracing climate of four thousand feet in the clouds. In its passage through these hills a series of rapids and long reaches of still water occur, and with the hills coming right down to the banks and rising abruptly thence, in places forest clad, in places scarped faces of quartzite rocks, crag over crag in regular steps, the scenery is singularly beautiful and quite equal to that of the Rhine. Even the ruins of ancient chateau and tower, which make the Rhine valley so interesting, are here simulated by the quartzite rocks, which are jointed vertically and horizontally, so that they stand out as great towers and buttressed walls, very like the battlements of some ancient fortress. A run down the river from Champa, where it enters the mountains, to Durjung, where the valley begins to broaden out, is well worth doing in March and April, when the river is low, and the waters of a deep-blue. During the rains, or when the river is full, this cannot be done, owing to the rapids being too dangerous. The sturdy Jhora boatmen shoot the rapids fearlessly in their dug-outs during the dry months.

One of the reaches of still water in this valley is known locally as *Mugger Gagra* (crocodile pool). This is a small lake about half-a-mile long, one hundred and fifty yards wide, and many fathoms deep. A low sand bar stretches along the left bank, and it is this bank that is a favourite breeding place for the *gharial*, or long-nosed crocodile.

At the time of my visit dozens of these great saurians were basking in the sun on the sand bar on the left bank. They allowed us to approach within twenty yards without making any attempt to move. Our guides said they were females watching over their eggs, which were buried in the sand. We threw several stones at them from the bank above, but they merely snapped their jaws viciously and made a loud hissing sound. They were of a fine slate-blue colour on all the exposed parts, and a creamy white below. The long snout, terminating in a saucer-like enlargement, is the most curious part of this strange animal. The jaw, at its thinnest part, is not more than nine inches round, and the snout terminates in a ball about six inches in diameter. Two males shot during the day measured respectively nineteen feet four inches and eighteen feet six inches, the massive tail making up fully one-third of the bulk.

When we had irritated the females (all small animals under twelve feet) for some time, they began to give off a strong musky odour. This, our Kol guides told us, was to call the bull crocodiles, and true enough, shortly afterwards we saw several of these monsters in the middle of the pool, with just the point of the snout and the dorsal ridge appearing above the surface, but from the height at which we stood we could see their great length in the clear water. Presently the water seemed quite alive with crocodiles, and two monsters showed themselves on the opposite bank. It was of no use shooting at the brutes in the water, as so little of them was to be seen above the surface; so, sighting my Martini for one hundred and fifty yards, I aimed carefully behind the shoulder of one and fired. Ere the echoes from the neighbouring hills had ceased, the sand bank was quite clear of the great lizards, the unaccustomed sound of the explosion sending them tumultuously into the deep water. I could see that my shot had taken effect on the opposite bank, as there was a great splashing of water, and every minute or two a great brute would come to the surface and raise his jaws quite clear of the water and snap them viciously together. This occurred several times, and then he drew himself up on to a rock on the opposite bank and there snapped and snapped his teeth for fully five minutes, when he died.

In the meantime a second large bull swam to the sand bar just below us, and with his body half out of the water kept watching us with his small fishy eyes. I and my friend fired together, and both our bullets took effect. He was into the water with a splash, and we saw no more of him till next day, when we found him lying dead on the sand bar. The creatures had now become more wary, and would not show themselves on land, although they kept swimming about in the pool not fifty yards off. We fired repeatedly at them in the water, but failed to drive them off, and the boatmen declared it would be dangerous to cross in the dug-out, as the animals would be certain to attack us if we entered the water. We had to walk back to camp at Durjung, three miles away, and come next day to recover our spoil. The brute first shot was a monster bull with a body larger round than a big buffalo's. He had one hundred and ninety-six teeth (large and small) in his jaws. According to the natives, these creatures have sixty-four teeth when young, and get four fresh teeth every year. If this assertion be true, then this brute must have been thirty-three years old, and since they are said to live often to a hundred years, what a row of teeth such a hoary monster would have!

The cork-like substance on the top of the round saucer nose was secured by the Kols as medicine. The fat also was carefully saved, and boiled down into oil, which finds a ready sale all over Bengal among native women as a sovereign remedy for sterility. It took a large amount of curing before the skins were fit to hang up. For the curing we used wheat, ground to a flour with all bran and husk, boiled with skimmed milk and made into a paste with other ingredients, in the following proportions: wheatmeal, 2 lbs.; alum, 1 lb.; wood-ashes, 2 lbs.; skimmed milk, 4 quarts; water, 4 quarts. This paste was rubbed in night and morning for a fortnight, when the skins became soft and free from smell.

WILD ELEPHANTS BY TRAIN.

THERE is no wild animal that takes to captivity so kindly as the lordly elephant. An elephant farm is an unknown institution. It is even very generally doubted whether these huge animals breed in captivity; but instances have been recorded where domesticated females have had young, although the instances are so few that there appears to be reason for the accepted belief. As far back as recorded history, it can be shown that the elephant was the servant of man. Some of the earlier Egyptian inscriptions, going back to B.C. 3,000 years, exhibit the elephant as a beast of carriage, and, strangely enough, these early drawings all depict the Asiatic variety, although Africa produces the lordly pachyderm in enormous numbers. That the African elephant has been tamed we know, from the fact of his having been used in the triumphal processions of several of the Roman emperors and generals. Thus, though thousands and hundreds of thousands of these animals have done man service, yet their ranks have always been recruited by capture from the herds of wild elephants that roam the forests of tropical Asia and Africa. Now, if the difficulty of training these creatures were at all in proportion to their size, a domesticated elephant would be a rarity; but the ease with which they can be broken into service, and the very great value of these services, account for their wholesale slavery from time immemorial. Eliminate from a captured herd all elephants above forty years of age, and in a fortnight's time the others will be amenable to discipline, and in a month may be set to work. I have given, in a previous chapter, some account of the capture of a herd of thirty-seven wild elephants in the presence of the late Duke of Clarence, when he visited Mysore in 1889. Within six weeks of their capture, most of them were sufficiently broken in to permit of their being brought into Bangalore and sent by rail to Calicut on the Malabar coast, where these animals are much in demand to work the timber forests.

At the Bangalore Railway station a large crowd had assembled to witness the transference into trucks of these unwieldy monsters. It was expected that the half-trained brutes would give some trouble before they could be got into the wagons intended to convey them to Calicut. About a dozen of them were tethered in a mango tope near the station, and when I saw them they did not show the least uneasiness at the crowds of human beings gathered around them. While watching a young tusker regaling himself on a bundle of sugar-cane, I suddenly felt something cold and clammy encircling my neck

THE RAJAH OF COOCH BEHAR'S FIGHTING ELEPHANTS.

[*To face page* 210.

from behind. I sprang forward in alarm, and turning round was horrified to see, as I momentarily thought, the expanded hood of a huge cobra elevated above a small enclosure near which I had been standing. Fortunately, however, there was no cobra; and on closer inspection I saw a number of baby elephants within the enclosure, and one of these little creatures had put its trunk over and was feeling me round the neck, when I started forward in such alarm. There were five of these babies, all under a year old, and standing about the height of a donkey. All the mothers had been shot, as too old for work, so that the little ones, deprived of their natural nourishment, were fed on boiled rice and milk poured down their throats from hollow bamboo vessels. It was amusing to see the little things curl up their trunks and elevate their mouths, so that the pap might be poured in without losing a drop. Quite a bucketful is a square meal, and this they indulge in twice a day. The preparations at the station were now sufficiently advanced, and a great *muckna* (tuskless male elephant) was the first taken to the siding to be entrained. Specially strengthened horse-trucks, with the tops and partitions removed, had been got ready by the Railway authorities for their transport. A strong gangway led from the platform into the truck, and the *mahout* (driver) was endeavouring to get the *muckna* over this and into the wagon, but without success. Nothing would induce him to go further than the entrance of the gangway.

No amount of coaxing, no amount of goading, could get him to advance a single step. More than an hour had been wasted in these vain endeavours, and then someone suggested that a hawser should be fitted round him, and that he should be dragged bodily into the truck. The hawser was adjusted, and fifty coolies started pulling. Step by step he was dragged half-way across the gangway. A shout of triumph went up from the spectators. Alas for their hopes! That very shout dashed them to the ground. Apparently alarmed at the noise, the elephant backed suddenly, and sent all the coolies sprawling on their faces. A windlass was next tried, but had to be given up, as the brute, finding his strength of no avail against the machine, turned himself sideways and jammed his body against the entrance of the gangway, so that he could not be pulled further without upsetting both gangway and truck.

The whole morning had now been wasted, and not a single animal had been got into the trucks provided for them. Many of the spectators had gone away disappointed. Mr. Sanderson, the famous *hathee* (elephant) king, who was in charge of the operations, was in despair, when a drunken *mahout* came forward and offered to get the elephants aboard if he were given a bottle of arrack (country spirit) as a present. Although doubting the man's ability to do what he undertook, the arrack was readily promised, and the *mahout* set to work at once. He directed two tame elephants to be brought up, and placed one on each side of the *muckna*. All three were then led up to the entrance of the gangway, the *muckna* in the centre, facing the entrance. A huge commissariat tusker now took up a position behind him, and at a word from its *mahout*, gave the *muckna* a prod in the stern with its tusks, and pushed him bodily forward. A scream of rage and fear burst from the recalcitrant beast, and he endeavoured to turn round, but found himself hemmed in by the mountains of flesh on either side of him. Another word from the *mahout*, and another prod from the tusker sent him half-way across the gangway. A third push, and he was safely landed within the truck, the tusker keeping guard at the entrance while the *muckna* was being hobbled and the door of the truck made secure. A shout of approval went up from the spectators, and many rupees and half-rupees fell to the drunken *mahout* for his clever, yet simple and effectual, method of overcoming recalcitrant elephants. By adopting the same means, in a very little time the whole batch were safely within the train and on their way to their destination.

THE *DHOLE*, OR WILD DOG.

NATURALISTS recognize but one species of wild-dog (*Cuon rutilans*) in India, but there can be no doubt there is a very great dissimilarity between the varieties noticed in different parts of the Peninsula. The *dhole*, or red dog, is found in the uplands and hill-tracts. In size not much larger than the common jackal, it is of an orange-red colour shading off to yellow under the stomach. It is of very slender build, and is shaped like a hound. It hunts by the scent, and is very courageous and tenacious of purpose. When once on the scent, it will follow up its quarry with the utmost determination, pursuing it for days until, utterly wearied out, it falls an easy victim to the pack.

A second variety of wild dog is found in the large stretches of forest at the foot of the various ranges of hills. It is more than double the size of the *dhole*, and of a lighter orange colour, flecked with grey along the back and tail. It is of a different build from the *dhole*, being more massive in the shoulder and loins. It is a splendid water dog, and will swim the largest rivers when in flood, and attack cattle in the water. This variety is very common in Assam, the Terai, and the Central Provinces. There is also a third, or intermediate, variety, from which the village or pariah dog is said to be descended.

The *dhole*, or red dog, is the most dreaded by the natives, and many are the stories they tell of its ferocity and determination. They say it will even attack the tiger and drive it off from its kill. The *dholes* hunt in packs of from six to eight (members of one family—parents and pups), but several packs have been known to combine to run down large game, such as a cow-bison with a very young calf, or an aged buffalo. I was once witness of an attack of the wild dog on a solitary wild buffalo of the largest size, and from what I then saw I can well believe many of the native stories of the courage and determination of these creatures.

We were encamped in an open glade in the great elephant forest of Jorda, about fifteen miles west of the town of Bonai, in Chota Nagpore. It was early morning, and the table for *chota hazri* (early breakfast) was laid outside the tent, when, while partaking of tea, we heard an occasional "yap! yap!" in the forest some distance away. On inquiry the native trackers told us that the sound proceeded from wild dogs on the trail, and that they were following up game of some kind, most probably a sambhur. The noise approached nearer and nearer, until now there was a great rustling in the forest and a magnificent bull-buffalo trotted leisurely into the glade. When he caught sight of the tents he stopped suddenly, and began pawing the ground, and threw up great tufts of grass and earth with side thrusts of his wide-spreading horns. There was an immediate scramble for guns, as we knew what that meant, and we hoped to be able to turn him with a well-directed shot before he wrecked our tents and furniture. We had not been a minute getting our guns, and had rushed out, momentarily expecting the buffalo to charge, when a strange sight presented itself. As if by magic, the bull was surrounded by a pack of fourteen *dholes*. They did not appear to be larger than half-grown setter puppies, and looked even smaller by the side of the great brute they had surrounded. How they were going to attack this enormous creature, or what chance they could have against its formidable horns and giant strength, we were curious to know, and watched the scene with great interest. The dogs took not the slightest notice of us, but kept circling round and round the buffalo and avoiding his charges with great skill. We soon noticed that all their feints of attack were directed to one side, so as to draw him into some low brushwood to the south of the glade. Our *shikarees* said this manœuvre to get their victim among the brushwood was for the purpose of blinding him; the dogs would micturate on the bushes, and then, when he charged with lowered head, their acrid urine on the leaves would get into his eyes and cause great irritation, so that he would be partially blinded, and they could attack him without fear. Sure enough, in a little time the buffalo was lured among the brushwood, and then we actually saw the dogs urinating on the bushes all around him. Charge after charge the buffalo made, but he never seemed to get up to his agile foes, who bounded out of reach of the great swinging horns. The bull did not make the slightest attempt to run, but would charge here, and then there, at his ever retreating, yet ever present, foes. The ground was scored up in every direction by the furious lunges of the great brute. Bushes were torn up by the roots, and sent flying in the air; yet not a casualty had occurred among his wily foes. We soon saw that there was some truth in what the *shikarees* had told us of the strange method the wild dog has of crippling its victim. I had often heard of this habit in the *dhole*, but had never credited it; yet here was the buffalo rubbing his eyes violently against his knees, springing into the air, and tossing about in a fury of agony. There could be no doubt that his eyes were affected, as he now began to charge blindly, and stumbled and fell repeatedly. We now approached nearer, as there was no danger from the buffalo, who seemed intent only on his canine foes, who had redoubled their activity, and no longer feinted, but made actual attacks on their huge opponent now that they saw he was blinded. We noticed, too, that all their assaults were delivered in the same spot, *viz.*, under the stomach of the buffalo, and that the scrotum was entirely torn away, and the poor brute bleeding to death. This is the favourite method of attack with wild dogs when attacking buffalo, bison, domestic oxen, and deer of all kinds. Indeed, in no other way would they be able to overcome these thick-skinned animals, as the tiny jaw of the wild dog would not be able to inflict fatal wounds in any other part.

Very soon the buffalo became exhausted from loss of blood, and sat down on his haunches. The dogs now became more audacious, and one actually pinned the buffalo by the nose. In a moment, with one stroke of its great hoof, the dog was struck dead, and the buffalo sprang to its feet, and kept stamping the body of the *dhole* to a pulp. Now it went on its knees, and kneaded the mass into the ground; and although the other dogs were tearing at its vitals, it took not the slightest notice, but seemed bent on wreaking its vengeance on the one which had fallen into its power. We thought it now time to interfere. A shot in the shoulder sent the bull forward a dozen paces in a wild charge; a second shot in the neck, and he fell dead. The dogs took to flight at the first shot, but seemed inclined to return when they saw the bull drop. A couple of charges of SS., and two of their number bit the dust, and the remainder scampered off.

It was singular that during all this fight, which lasted more than half an hour, the dogs had not given tongue in the least. Neither bark nor growl had escaped them. The buffalo frequently roared with rage. There is no other term for the cry of an infuriated buffalo. It is certainly not a bellow, nor is it a grunt, but is very like the roar of a tiger when charging. We now had time to examine the buffalo. It was a magnificent beast, in its prime. The spread of the horns was enormous, quite twelve feet from tip to tip, measured round the curve. The *dholes* had torn the poor creature's genitals completely out; both scrotum and testes were gone, so that death would have occurred in a little time if we had not shot it. I don't know whether any other writer on *shikar* has noticed this peculiar method of attack by wild dogs. I have seen it stated that they generally make for the eye and seize their prey there. Some say that they make for the heels, and hamstring their quarry; but I have invariably noticed in deer, buffalo, and bison that have been run down by wild dogs that the genitals have been the place of attack. Only three weeks ago, a young sambhur was run down by a pair of wild dogs near my camp. The poor brute ran in among the coolies, who drove off the dogs and secured the sambhur, but it had to be killed, as the genitals were almost torn out and it would have died in a short time.

A friend of mine, a coffee planter in the Wynaad, once had a pair of *dhole* puppies brought him by the coolies. Although only just able to run about, the foxy smell from them was so intolerable that no amount of washing would remove it, and they had to be sent away from the bungalow and lodged in the hen-house. My friend succeeded in rearing the slut, and from her he got a litter of puppies from a cross with a half-bred Poligar. When she was big with pup, she disappeared for some time, and it was thought that a leopard had carried her off. Some of the servants declared, however, that they saw her about at night. In a little time the fowls began to disappear mysteriously. Nearly every morning a good fat hen would be missing. The servants were set on the watch, and Junglee, as the bitch was called, was soon seen in the act of seizing a hen and running off in the direction of a large stack of timber. A careful search was made, and a burrow ten feet in length, driven clean under the timber, was discovered. The timber was removed and the burrow dug out, and six pups about three weeks old were discovered among a heap of feathers. Junglee had to be chained up, as she several times made attempts to carry off and conceal her pups. I secured one of the pups; he turned out a large and powerful dog, double the size of his mother, but with all her keen powers of scent and alertness of movement, and with the shoulders and weight of his Poligar father. He was one of the best sporting dogs I ever had, and was an invaluable companion in the jungle. He always gave notice of game long before it could be seen, by a peculiar low whine, which could not be heard more than a few yards off, and by the erection of the hair along his back. His only failing was want of voice, as he would never give tongue when following a scent, or even when he brought the game to bay; but this was soon remedied by giving him a pariah dog as a companion. This was a most cowardly brute that would not approach within twenty yards of any animal brought to bay by Tiger (the half-breed *dhole*), but he barked most vociferously, and thus gave notice of the whereabouts of Tiger and game. Tiger would attack anything under the sun, if ordered to do so—a snake or an elephant, it was all the same; he knew no fear. He was only wounded on one occasion, and then by a mongoose. He, too, always directed his attacks on the same place as did the *dholes*, and, like them, he was without voice, beyond an occasional whine.

In a former chapter I gave an account of the remarkable powers of swimming of the larger grey variety of wild dog. On that occasion, the reader will remember, a couple of these creatures breasted the Koel river when in flood, and kept ahead of a dug-out paddled by two powerful boatmen. What was more astonishing still, they did this even down stream, and kept up the pace for over a mile, diving on several occasions to avoid my shots. The tails of this variety are extremely long, with a large tuft of strong hair at the end. This they use as a kind of propeller when swimming. It also enables them to turn readily in the water, and is of material use when diving. I don't know whether this kind of *dhole* hunt by scent or merely course like the greyhound. That they have means of communicating with each other, and can concert a regular plan of attack, is evident from the following incident.

We had just ascended some rising ground overlooking a stretch of scrub jungle extending as far as the left bank of the Koel, when our attention was drawn to a pack of four wild dogs squatted on their haunches, close together, and evidently watching something in the scrub towards the river. Their backs were towards us, so we had time to conceal ourselves and watch their further movements. Now and again one of the group would leave its companions, make a short reconnoitre, and return with information which it evidently imparted to its fellows. In a little time two of the dogs set off, one in a direction down stream, and the other up; the other two separated a few hundred yards, but without advancing towards the game they had evidently spotted. About ten minutes after the dogs had gone up and down stream, one of those that had remained behind rushed forward into the scrub and roused a fine stag sambhur (*C. Aristotelis*) that must have been lying up in a dense cover of scrub. The stag at once made off down stream, the dog pursuing for a hundred yards or so and then returning to the place whence it started. For a little time the sambhur had disappeared from view, and we were about to resume our journey, when we saw him in the distance making back with a wild dog in hot pursuit. Now the sambhur headed up stream, the dog following a few hundred yards and then lying close. We began to understand the tactics of the dogs, but still did not take in all the details, so waited to see the *dénouement*. The stag must have made up stream until he was turned by the dog we saw go off in that direction, as we now saw him returning with the dog close at his heels. The chase was not long continued, as this dog also stopped short and concealed itself, while the now thoroughly alarmed deer continued its headlong flight till within a hundred yards of the spot where the dog down stream had concealed itself,when it sprang into view and caused the stag to swerve away to the left, until again turned by one of the dogs concealed in that direction. The now thoroughly bewildered brute began running round and round in a gradually narrowing compass, as at each point he was met and turned by one of his adversaries, who advanced a little way and then stopped. The stag made repeated and ineffectual attempts to break away up and down stream and to the left, but on every occasion it was headed by the dogs concealed in those directions and driven back. We thought it was the plan of the dogs to thoroughly tire the sambhur out, and then fall upon him; yet, this could scarcely be their object, as the direction of the river was left quite open, and to this point the hunt was evidently making. Closer and closer drew the cordon of ever-watchful dogs, husbanding their strength for the *finale*, which now could not be far off, as the river was in view and the gradually lessening space allowed the affrighted deer was now not more than an acre or two. We hurried up to be in at the death, when we saw the stag make a bound and disappear into the river, all four dogs in close pursuit. When we got to the banks we saw the sambhur in deep water with a dog hanging on to each ear, and two hanging on to his tail. We soon made out that the object of the dogs was to keep the brute in deep water, for they pulled with all their strength whenever he attempted to swim in the direction of a sand-bank in the river, as they probably knew that if he got into shallow water he would be more than a match for them, since he would be able to use his feet and antlers when the water would still be too deep for them to escape his attack. Now and again one of the dogs at his tail would dive down and attack his groin, when the sambhur would throw up his haunches to avoid his antagonist; the dogs at the ears would seize this moment to drag his head under water and keep it there till he was nearly suffocated. The dogs were in much better wind, as they had done little or no chasing, while the stag was nearly done with the long coursing he had undergone from point to point. After three or four unsuccessful attempts to drown the poor brute, his efforts to shake off his foes becoming weaker and weaker, he was at length overcome and kept under so long that when the dogs re-appeared at the surface and actually towed him by the ears till near the sand-bank, he made no movement and we knew he was dead. They now took him by the tail and drew the body partly out of the water and began feasting on his groin, which we saw was dreadfully lacerated by their attacks when in the water. My men were now for interfering, but I would not permit them, as I thought the dogs deserved their meal for their very clever scheme for capturing a brute so much larger and stronger than themselves. It was not until the dogs had had a surfeit that I allowed such of my servants as chose to take any of the flesh.

A TIGER IN THE NETS.

PERHAPS one of the strangest methods of hunting tigers is by capturing them in nets, and when so entangled, spearing them to death. That this method of capture dates from very early times we have evidence in the fable of the Lion and the Mouse, which is undoubtedly of Indian origin, being founded on the beast fables of the *Pancha Tantra*, one of the oldest Sanskrit books.

It is hard to conceive so large and ferocious an animal as a tiger, with his strong teeth and sharp claws, imprisoned in so frail a contrivance as a mesh of fine cords. One would think that with a single bound he would break and be through them; or that with his sharp teeth he would quickly sever the thin cords to shreds. But it is just this inability to bound, with the entangling skeins of the net clogging all his limbs, and the uselessness of biting through a single mesh when the very effort brings fifty other meshes round his ears, that makes him fall an easy victim to the treacherous net, and keeps him a fast prisoner till the arrival of his human foes, who make short work of him with their spears, since he is unable to offer the least show of fight, so hampered is he with the folds of the light yet strong fabric of the nets. This method of destroying the dread monster may sound unsportsmanlike to English ears; but the Indian does not hunt for sport. With him the destruction of animals that prey on his flocks and herds is a stern necessity, and any means of getting rid of such creatures is justifiable.

I know of only one part of India where tigers are still captured in nets. In the Wynaad, a part of the Malabar district on the west coast of South India, the natives employ this method of entrapping and killing tigers, which are very numerous and destructive on the forest-clad hills and valleys that make up the bulk of this region. In the uplands abutting on the coastal reaches are long, low, marshy valleys, where much rice is grown by a race of people called Chetties. These are the landlords of the soil, and each Chetty owns a number of Punniar slaves (a dark squat race of the negroid type), who do most of the hard work and who are bought and sold with the land, as a kind of fixture, the number of such slaves materially increasing the value of the paddy flat. The Chetties are, in fact, a fine race of men, tall and fair, with clean-cut features of the Aryan type. They are extremely hospitable, open, and free in their manners, dearly loving a *lotah* of palm-wine (toddy), which they tap from the talipot palms that are usually found near their dwellings, and not unwilling to share it with the planter Sahibs whose coffee estates dot the hill-sides for miles round.

I was camped near a paddy flat some seven miles from Gudaloor on the Sultan's Battery Road in South East Wynaad, when, early one morning in March, a fine old Chetty called at my tent and wished to know whether the *doray* (gentleman) would like to see a tiger which was caught in the nets the previous night. Of course the *doray* was only too willing to witness so novel a sight, so off we set, I taking the precaution to carry with me a gun in case of emergency.

The nets are about twelve feet wide and thirty yards long, with four-inch meshes. They are made of quarter-inch cord of green cocoanut fibre, which is immensely strong. A stronger cord passes through the top and bottom of the length of the net. There are two methods of using these nets. When a tiger has killed a cow or bullock, his lair for the time, which is generally near to his kill, is marked down and is surrounded by beaters from all the neighbouring villages. One path alone is left open, and across this the nets are stretched. The lower rope of the net, which runs along the ground, is fastened to pegs on either side of the path. The top rope is loosely supported on bamboo uprights, at intervals of a few yards, which spread out the net and make a fragile and scarcely perceptible barrier across the unguarded space. The uprights are so lightly fitted that the slightest pressure on the net knocks them away and the whole net comes to the ground, covering the creature that attempts to force its way through. When all is ready a frightful din begins ; all the beaters shouting and screaming at the top of their voices and clashing every noise-making utensil they can get hold of. The tiger roused from his sleep after a full meal, hears the noise approaching him from all sides but one. He makes in that direction, and scarcely notices the thin netting barring his way. He presses against the meshes and down the uprights go, the net falling on him and enclosing him in its folds. On feeling the net over him he makes a few frantic bounds, which only serve to pull out the pegs to which the lower rope is fastened, and bring the ends together so as to completely envelop him. If left to himself he might probably be able to bite through the meshes in time and free himself, but the spearsmen, who have been concealed in the branches of the neighbouring trees, are quickly on the spot and dispatch him with thrusts of their long-handled spears.

Kills are not of every-day occurrence, and are rather expensive items to the unfortunate owner of the beast, so that this kind of beat into the nets is uncommon. The more usual practice is to set the nets across some known track of the tiger, either to the spot where he drinks water or where he prowls round the cattle pen. In this case the nets are placed three deep with intervals of a yard. His struggles when he brings the first net down on himself, bring him within the toils of the second, and perhaps of the third, so that he is a fast prisoner till the men arrive next morning and dispatch him.

This was the position of the tiger on the morning the Chetty came for me. When we arrived at the village, every soul was afoot, and our appearance was the signal for a vigorous beating of tomtoms, to which the spearsmen of the village did a kind of war-dance, circling round and round the pole, in the centre of the threshing-floor, to which the cattle are attached when treading out the corn. The spears were most murderous-looking weapons, with blades a foot long and bamboo handles twelve feet in length. The Punniars were not allowed to use the spear; only Chetties were so armed. The spear handles were marked with stripes of turmeric, in honour of the occasion. We now moved off to the scene of the capture, which was near to the cattle pens. The drummers, who were Punniars, beat vigorously on a long, barrel-shaped drum, each head of which was strung to give a different note, and as this pitch could be varied by pressure of the hands on the drum-head, a sort of rhythmic measure was kept up, to which the spearsmen danced in their onward march. The women were not allowed to follow the procession. On arrival at the scene, the spectators formed a wide circle around what appeared to me a mass of cordage inextricably entangled. The spearsmen lined the inner front of the circle and kept back the crowd, who were armed with axes, reaping-hooks, stout sticks, rice-beaters, etc. I was told I could enter the circle and examine the tiger, as there was no danger. On our approach there was a subdued growl, with a convulsive movement of the cordage, as the only signs that the tiger was within the network of ropes. Probably the brute had quite exhausted himself in his previous efforts to shake off the nets. Successive prods with the blunt end of the spear failed to elicit more than a savage growl. I suggested that they should throw a pail of water over the brute, as the cold douche might rouse him, but to this the Chetties objected. "It was not the custom," they said, and they are great sticklers for custom.

We were now told to stand back, as the Slaying Ceremonies were about to begin. The drums renewed their thumping, when the chief Chetty stepped into the ring with spear in hand and began a kind of step dance. With legs outspread he made a complete circuit of the enclosure, measuring off the distance as one would with a drawing compass. Now commenced a series of hops on one foot and feints and lunges with the spear. Soon he was joined by a second and a third, and so on to a sixth spearsman, all of whom did exactly like their leader. Now they divided into two parties on opposite sides of the circle and cut the same antics. Rushes were made with levelled spears at the inert body in the centre, but these were only feints to rouse the tiger. Then all was silent and the leader of the Chetties began apostrophizing the tiger, and wished to know if that was the *na-andamaganay* (son of a dog) that frightened the old women and ran off with their cattle. "Yes! yes!" shouted the multitude, "that is he!" "Is that the thief who would not show his face to the daylight, so that the sons of Ram might know him?" "Yes! yes!" shouted the mob again. "Is this the lord of the forest, the mighty one at whom even the elephant trembles?" "No! no! this is a dog and a son of a dog!" This abuse is kept up for some time, and then the leader says: "Ye mighty ones of Pursuram, show what you do with stealers of cattle, frighteners of old women, and prowlers of the night." There is silence for a moment. The six spearsmen range themselves, three on each side, with spears levelled at the object in the centre. Suddenly there is a loud thump of the drums, and a shout from the multitude, as the six spearsmen rush forward and thrust their spears simultaneously into the body of the tiger. With a mighty effort the tiger brings his legs together and springs clean into the air, nets and all; the upward bound sends the spearsmen sprawling, two of the spear handles snapping short off, while the others still stick in the body of the tiger like the quills of a porcupine. Now the mob rush forward and begin belabouring the body, till all signs of life are extinct. The spears are withdrawn, and boys over a certain age are marked across the chest with the blood of the tiger, as a sign of manhood. Then the nets are unloosened, and the body is carried in triumph to the village.

MY *SHIKAREE* FRIENDS.

IV.—FAZUL THE MAHOUT.

"How long have I been a *mahout?* As long as I know of—from a child I have been with elephants. My father, who is an old man, is still a *mahout*, and his father was before him. We are a family of *mahouts* for many generations back. My grandfather was *mahout* to one of the nobles of the Emperor of Delhi, and was present with his elephant at the battle of *Punputh* (Paniput). We are Rohillas by race, but have settled down in Behar these two generations. I am now in the service of the Sircar, but formerly I worked for the Raja of Durbhunga under whom my father is still employed.

"Elephants are like women—they cannot be trusted. When they appear most attached to you, then they meditate mischief. My uncle Oomer was killed by his elephant at Dacca. The fuss he made with that elephant! Twice a day he rubbed it down with a brick and painted its ears with vermilion and white. He spent half his wages on oil and *gur* and *metay* (sweet-stuff) for the wretch; yet in an evil hour it killed him. Why or wherefore, no one knows. Certainly it was sorry afterwards, and wept—yes, wept, Sahib; we saw the tears in its eyes; elephants cry. Ask any *mahout*; he will tell you. It is true words I am telling you. When my aunt saw her husband's dead body, she took up her infant son and threw it before the elephant and cried, 'Oh, wretch! you have taken the life of my life, now take that of my son also. You have eaten of our best and have had more attention than even I had from him whose life you have taken. Here is his son; kill him, I say, kill him!' That elephant was ashamed and cried and fondled the little one, and none dared take him from the brute but my aunt. Then it was told to Sanderson Sahib and he made the baby *mahout* in my uncle's place, and my aunt had charge of the elephant till the boy grew. Whenever my aunt went to the bazaar or was engaged cooking or about her household duties, she would make over her baby to the elephant to look after, and it was strange to watch how that great animal would fondle it with its trunk and whisk the flies off it and pull it out of the sun; and when he began to crawl it was fun to see the elephant take him by his leg and prevent him crawling away. None dared take the baby from the elephant but my aunt, and if the little one was not brought to it in the morning it would become restless and excited and would try to break its chain, and could only be appeased by the little fellow's presence. When my cousin grew old enough to run about and talk, the way he bullied that elephant was astonishing. He would get under its belly and prick it with thorns, he would pinch its trunk, he would remove sugar-cane from its mouth, but the great creature would only grunt its satisfaction. Sanderson Sahib would sit for hours and watch that elephant and boy at play; and he took their pictures. How is it my aunt took charge of the elephant after it killed her husband? That was his *nusseeb* (fate); who can help his fate? The elephant fed her child and herself after my uncle's death, therefore why should she not look after him? Yet still, for all, elephants are not to be trusted. I have lived my life with them, and I ought to know.

"No, Sahib, elephants are not clever; it is only with the *ankwas* (goad) that we can make them understand. The elephant is as the *mahout* is. If the latter is sharp, the elephant will do almost anything. Even a well-trained elephant grows dull under a stupid *mahout*. Sanderson Sahib used to say, 'Give me a good *mahout* and indifferent elephant rather than a clever elephant and stupid *mahout*.'

"Yes, I have been to Assam and Burmah; I have been in the Terai and in Mysore and Ceylon. I went to Mysore with Sanderson Sahib when the *Padishaw* (Duke of Clarence) came to India. We went to show them how to catch elephants. I was chief nooser, and the Lord Sahib spoke to me through the one-handed Sahib (Sir Charles Bradford). See, here is the certificate the one-armed Sahib gave me. We caught fifty elephants in the *kheddah* at Mysore when the *Padishaw* came. We took twelve *koonkies* (decoy elephants) with us from Dacca. Without *koonkies* elephants could not be secured when driven into the *kheddah*. There is no danger when on the *koonkies'* neck; the only danger is when we are hobbling the wild elephant's feet. If we are not quick with the noose, the brute will swing out its hind foot, and should it hit you, death or broken bones are certain to result.

"Where are the largest herds? Herds always number about the same, twenty to thirty, seldom more. The members of a herd are all of one family. There may be several herds in one district, but they never mingle; they always keep apart. If from any cause an elephant should become separated from its herd and try to join another, it won't be allowed to; the members will turn it out—hence the solitary elephants one sometimes sees. In the Garo Hills, in Assam, there are the most herds. In one season we caught four hundred and thirty elephants there. In Burmah also there are many herds. Sometimes two or three herds may be driven into a *kheddah* at one time, but these will always keep apart.

"Do wild elephants dance? *Wagh! Wagh!* What talk is this? Are elephants nautch-girls, that they should dance? Who has been lying to the Sahib? The Assamese and Kachees are liars and sons of liars if they say so. Yes, there are elephant-circles or cleared spaces in the heart of the forest, where no man has been, but these are the elephant meeting-places when they meet to go to a far country. When the bamboo leaves become black with leaf disease the elephants all leave that country and go away for a year or two, and then

ELEPHANTS MIGRATING.

[*To face page* 237.

come back. They do not go in single herds, but hundreds assemble at these meeting-places and talk and talk and then decide where they will go and how they will go. Yes, I have seen these meeting-places when out with Sanderson Sahib, but I have never witnessed a meeting. The Sahib must know that elephants are the most restless creatures in the world ; you can never get an elephant to stop perfectly quiet for five minutes. It will shift from leg to leg, fling its trunk about, flap its ears or shake its head. If not chained it will walk about, and never stand still in one place. When the elephants meet to take counsel when they shall leave the country, they cannot keep quiet but walk about in a circle—hence the open spaces in the forests. Moving about from foot to foot may look like dancing to the wild men. Yes, that is how they must say that elephants dance. The Sahib is wise. Only old elephants go to the meeting-places—the leaders of the herd, male or female. Why should not a female lead a herd ? Have you not got a Ranee ? I have seen herds led by a female, and such herds are always more difficult to capture, as we cannot send *koonkies* to decoy them. The *koonkies* are female elephants, and we always use them to decoy the tusker that leads the herd, and then the herd will follow him.

"Have I seen an elephant-fight ? Yes, often. During the *kheddah*-works in Assam we had to watch the herd of wild elephants night and day for months, and gradually drive them towards the valley in which the *kheddah* was made, and thus one sees much of elephant life and learns their ways when in the wild state. In the *uthee-khana* (elephant stables) the elephants are under control and are mostly grown animals, so one learns little of their natural habits. Three or four seasons in the jungle at *kheddah*-work and you learn a deal. When a young bull becomes *must* for the first time it always fights, generally with some other young tusker. It is only when the leader becomes very old or enfeebled from disease that he has to fight to maintain his place as leader. Then it is a fight to the death, or the challenger has to leave the herd and becomes the dangerous brute known as a solitary bull. When one young tusker wishes to fight another he challenges him by kicking dust in his face with his forelegs. When the challenge is accepted the remainder of the herd clear off some distance, and go on feeding without taking the slightest notice. The fighters face each other about twenty paces apart. They grunt and trumpet out defiance. Then they back a few paces like fighting rams, and rush at each other with heads lowered and trunks coiled between the forelegs. The shock is great, and should either be thrown the other immediately proceeds to kick the prostrate one until he gets up and runs away. They seldom stand a second charge, unless it be a fight between the leader and some aspirant for his post. Then tusks are used and great wounds are inflicted, and the battle lasts hours. The greatest fight I have seen was between two tame ones. Sanderson Sahib has put it in his book, so you may have seen it. I was *mahout* to Motee Goocha, the great fighting tusker at Dacca. We were up at *kheddah*-work in the north when Luxa, a large tusker we had caught the previous season, went *must* and killed Pichee, his Mug *mahout*. Pichee was a *baycoop* (fool). He drank *muddut* (smoked opium). When Luxa was *must*, instead of giving it the opium served out by the *jemadar* for *must*-elephants, Pichee stole it and made *muddut*. In his drunken fits he beat Luxa with a bamboo when taking it to water. Luxa stamped on him and killed him, and ran off into the jungles. We give our elephants twelve *seers* of paddy every day. In the jungles Luxa got no paddy, so it went to the villages at night and smelled out the place where the villagers keep the paddy in baskets in a corner of their huts. It would quietly pull off the thatch, put its trunk down into the basket and suck up its trunk full of paddy and blow the paddy into its mouth. After emptying the basket, it would go to another hut and do the same. One night while stealing paddy, the man of the house got up, and thinking there was a thief there he stabbed the elephant in its trunk with his spear. The elephant ran off with a scream and was not seen again for a week. The next time it came it pulled down the house and killed a couple of villagers, and when they all ran away it quietly took possession of the village and remained there till all the rice was eaten; then it would go off and attack another village.

"In this way it had killed many persons and looted several villages, when Sanderson Sahib determined to recapture it. Motee Goocha and two of the best *koonkies* were selected. The *jemadar*, Ali, and myself were the *mahouts*, and I drove Motee Goocha, with Sanderson Sahib on the pad behind me. A strong cable noose (lassoo) was on the neck before me, and made fast at the other end to Motee Goocha's girth. We were to go five miles, to a village which Luxa had looted that night. When we got near the village some of the villagers who were hiding in the forest told us that Luxa was still at the village eating paddy. Sanderson Sahib told the *jemadar* to keep the *koonkies* some distance behind, and while we were fighting Luxa they were to get behind and try and surround it, so that it could not run away. We went along quietly, I encouraging Motee Goocha the while, but he wanted no encouraging; he was only too ready for the fight. I could tell that by the feel of his jaws on my toes. With knees and feet, we *mahouts* can tell all the feelings of an elephant when we are seated behind its ears. Motee Goocha's were now worked convulsively, so I knew he scented a fight. The rogue watched us approach, but did not take any notice, as elephants see badly, and it did not perceive Sanderson Sahib or myself, but probably mistook Motee Goocha for a wild one. When we got within fifty yards it scented us and began trumpeting and screaming and kicking the dust towards us. It advanced a few paces as if to frighten us; and finding we still approached, it threw forward its ears, backed a few paces and then came on with a rush. '*Asthe, Bayta! Asthe!* (easy, my son! easy). Don't waste your breath on that son of a dog,' said I to Motee Goocha who was but too eager for the fray. When within ten paces Sanderson Sahib told me to shout to Luxa to stop and sit down, as runaway elephants frequently remember the words of command they have been accustomed to, and involuntarily obey. The sound of my voice seemed only to infuriate the rogue, for it only screamed the fiercer and continued to come on with head lowered and trunk coiled away. In these face-to-face charges elephants don't use their tusks until after the first shock is received on the thick frontal bone of the skull, otherwise the tusks would be broken clean off in the terrific force of two such enormous weights coming together with such speed. Forehead to forehead like two rams came they together, and both were thrown back on their haunches by the dreadful shock. Recovering themselves they both backed several paces and looked at each other a moment, and then to it again, but this time not so fast as the first charge. Trunks were now entwined and each tried to lift the other's head, so as to get at the chest and deliver a fatal thrust with the tusks. Now they reared on their hind legs like two horses, and continued the struggle with their trunks. Sanderson Sahib was thrown off the pad at this time by the unexpected movement of Motee Goocha rising on his hind legs. Luxa was the taller beast, and when on his hinds Motee Goocha's head was below that of the runaway, and he was able to get his opponent's neck between his tusks and with a dexterous twist he threw it on its side. In a moment my noose was over the fore-foot and I felt sure of the brute. Urging Motee Goocha close up, he kept Luxa down with his tusks while Sanderson Sahib shackled the hind legs of the rogue. The *koonkies* now came up, and Luxa thoroughly cowed was allowed to rise. With great difficulty a hawser was fastened round its neck and lashed to the *koonkies*, one on each side, so that it could not run away without dragging the *koonkies* with it. A prod or two from Motee Goocha's tusk applied behind soon set it in motion, and thus we rode home in triumph. Luxa turned out a first-rate elephant after that, and did a lot of good work. Whenever it showed temper, the very sight of Motee Goocha reduced it to order. That was the grandest elephant fight I ever saw."

A BIG SNAKE.

SOME years ago we were at Sumpta, a part of the Sarunda State Forest, Chota Nagpore, seeing to the marking of *sâl* trees to be cut down for sleepers which the Forest Department had undertaken to supply to the Oudh and Rohilkund Railway. The heat was intense, something like 114° in the shade, so that even the physical training of a Cooper's Hill course, where physical fitness is a *sine quâ non*, had to admit itself beaten and prefer a siesta in the shade to a ten-mile tramp over hill and dale even after the largest of solitary bison. Our coolies had come in with reports of a solitary bull here, a cow and a calf there, or a herd somewhere else, all within easy march; but bison-shooting meant a day or two away from duty, and our Chief C—— was a devil for work, and thought more of a sleeper or two brought to the railway station than bagging the biggest tusker in Singbhoom, or the record horns of a bull bison.

We were talking of school-days and of football matches, and arguing whether M. or S. was not the best half-back of his year and entitled to a place in any county fifteen, when my servant

Karim interrupted our reminiscences of Cooper's Hill with "*Sahib! coolie loka boltha burra samp hai pad may najeek* (coolies say there is a large snake in the hill near)." With all the ardour of schoolboys we sprang to our feet, forgetting the sweltering sun and our half-told tales of school-life, and set off at a run to scotch the snake. The old Hebrew writer was correct, I think, so far as Eve's descendants were concerned: "I will put enmity between thy seed and her seed." The horror and detestation of a snake is pretty general among human beings; at least I can answer for myself. Taking my shot-gun with me, we hurried off with our informants, who stated that they had just seen a monster snake, as large and as thick as a *sal* tree, take refuge in a cave among some rocks on a neighbouring height. S——g declared it must be an *Ophiophagus elaps*, or King-Cobra, of which a specimen had been seen in these parts. He declared he was acquainted with the forest of Singbhoom and there were no boas in the district. I was new to the country so could not offer an opinion either way, and was only half-inclined to go for our friend the King-Cobra after the dreadful accounts I had heard of the ferocity and deadliness of that monster snake. The natives however said it was not a *nag* (cobra), and after seeing the cave—a mere hole about a foot or more wide—I was more inclined to think it an iguana, common in these parts. But peering in at the entrance, we could make out the great coils of an enormous snake round a projecting rock in the further part of the chamber, under the overhanging rocks. The coolies were posted with *lathies* and axes along the passage the snake was likely to take, while I endeavoured to dislodge him with a shot in the body; no sign of his head could be seen. Telling the men to be careful of his rush should he be a King-Cobra, I fired into the cave and then bolted to one side.

Not a stir or rustle to show that the shot had taken effect, neither did the reptile—whatever it was—charge out of the hole. When the smoke had cleared away we could still see the coils round the rock, and fancying the snake was dead we got a long stick with a crook at the end and endeavoured to haul it out; but the united efforts of six of us could not move it an inch. Beyond an occasional hiss, the monster gave no other signs of life than a convulsive clinging to the rock round which it had thrown its folds. I now tried the effects of a second shot, aiming with great care at the body, as I was inclined to think my first shot had missed. There was no doubt that this shot had gone home, as the brute at once uncoiled and made for the entrance; but the sight of so many foes ready to do battle, sent it back to its shelter again. A third shot, and this time the creature was fairly out of the hole and making down-hill at good speed, the coolies belabouring it with clubs. We now saw that it was a rock snake or boa, common to many parts of India, and non-poisonous. Finding itself hard pressed by its human foes, the creature turned round and again made for its hole, and, in spite of the merciless belabouring it got with great sticks, it had nearly reached its shelter when S——g rushed forward and seizing it by the tail, which he placed over his shoulder, and turning his face downhill, began hauling away as if at a great cable. More than half its body was now off the ground, so that the creature could not obtain a purchase, yet it struggled hard and S——g swayed and shook with each movement of its great body, and I expected momentarily to see him knocked to the ground or in the coils of the gigantic brute. But his football experience stood him in good stead, and clinging to the tail of the serpent in regular Rugby style he struggled onwards, pulling the snake after him. A native now rushed up and split open its head with a battle-axe, and a fourth shot finished the fight.

Before skinning, it measured twelve feet two inches in length, and was about as thick round as the small of a man's thigh. We removed the skin, thinking to send it home to Cooper's Hill to show the fellows there what was expected of Foresters in India, but before morning there was but little of it left, for the ants having found their way up had played havoc with the whole carcase.

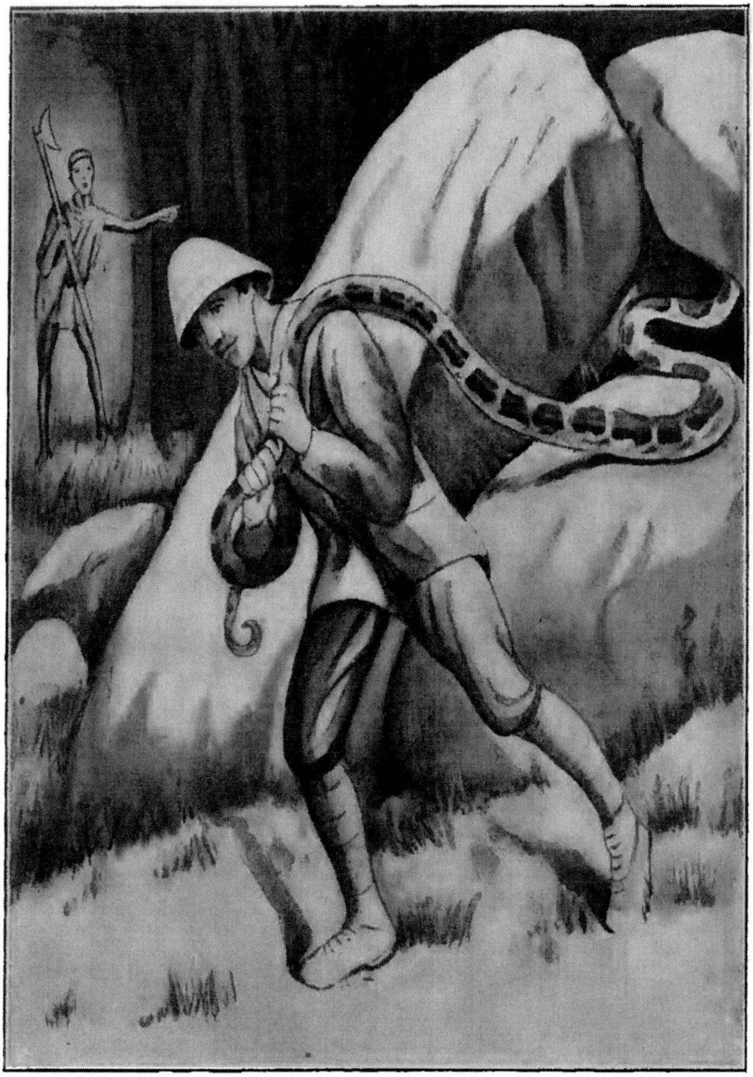

A BIG SNAKE.

[*To face page* 246.

AFTER BISON IN CHOTA NAGPORE.

It is not generally known that within a night's railway journey of Calcutta there is a shooting preserve where, on the payment of a fee of ten rupees a month, permission to shoot game of any kind but elephant can be had for the asking. The Saranda Reserved Forest covers some seven hundred miles of heavily-wooded country, alive with game of all kinds—buffalo, bison, deer, tiger, leopard, bear, pig, huge snakes and game birds. It is easy of access, as the Bengal-Nagpore Railway runs through it from Goilkora to Rourkela, and no part of it is more than twenty-five miles from a railway station. Excellent food supplies too can be had from Messrs. Kellner's Railway Refreshment Rooms at Chakardarpore. This fine shooting ground was little known, because the Forest Officers had come to regard it as their own little preserve, where they were sure of a bag whenever they were inclined for a day's shoot; or where a particular friend or two could be invited down during the holidays and treated to sport usually reserved for friends and acquaintances of Cooch Behar and other Rajas with shooting preserves. It is not long since Dr. P——, from Fort William, spent a few days here and bagged one of the finest solitary bison to be seen. He was out by himself with only a tracker or two, and came on the brute end on, and at twenty paces was able to put in a right and left from a heavy ten-bore, but the position was a bad one for a mortal shot, the bullets hitting high on the withers. The beast made off and put a mile of ground between itself and its pursuers before, overcome with the loss of blood, it sank down in the long grass to rest awhile. When first seen, the rain was coming down in torrents, so that P—— was able to get within twenty yards without difficulty; but after delivering his fire he was unable to get in two fresh cartridges, as the wet had swollen the cases and they jammed. The torrents of rain and the noise of the shower prevented the bison seeing from which direction the shot had come, or he might have charged and done some damage; so after sniffing the air awhile he made off down hill and took shelter in some heavy grass. It was some little time before P—— could reload his gun, and he then set off in search of the bison, which he was sure could not have gone very far after being so badly wounded. The tracks were plain and easily followed up, and the native *shikarees* soon pointed out the huge brute lying in a clump of grass. Two more shots, which were afterwards discovered to have taken effect in the region of the ribs, and the brute was up and away like the wind, receiving two hasty shots as he was scurrying through the grass. The rain now came down in torrents so that all sight of him was lost, and the tracks were washed out by the streams of water running down the hillside. Close search was made next day, but they were unable to find any trace of the bison and thought it lost for ever. P—— returned to Calcutta; but two days later the body of the bull was recovered miles away from the spot where he was last seen. The skin was quite spoilt; but the head was cut off and sent to P——, who was strongly enjoined not to tell where he had bagged the brute, or the whole of Saranda would be overrun with sportsmen from Fort William and the State Forest would no longer be the preserve it is.

The best places for *shikar* are to the south and east of the Manharpore railway station, and some eight miles away among the Ankua range of hills, for twenty miles south. At Thamsi, Phoolbari, and Hundagudi the country abounds with large game. There is not the slightest difficulty about trackers and *shikarees;* they can be had at all the native villages near the forest, while the railway stations make capital rest-camps. Provisions can be had from Chakardarpore daily if necessary, so that the usual discomforts of a long shooting trip and the heavy expenses of transport are not incurred if Saranda be the scene of the excursion. The jungles are not unhealthy during the wet months, and if one is provided with stout boots and a good waterproof there need be feared nothing beyond a good wetting now and again. The damp ground makes tracking simple work and game can be followed up more easily than in the dry weather. During the hot months it is more difficult to obtain a permit, as there is always the danger of forest fires from a lighted end of a cigar, or from camp fires. All things considered the monsoon is about the best time for shooting within the forest reserve.

The native *shikarees* dread the solitary bull-bison, and will if possible lead the hunter off the track and take him to a herd of several cows and calves, with perhaps a young bull as master of the herd. The solitary bulls are generally aged animals, no longer fit to rule the herd, and ousted perhaps by some younger rival. It is hard to say why the natives dread this animal, as unlike the solitary buffalo he will not attack unless molested, and always endeavours to make off unless brought to bay at close quarters.

Some years ago I saw one of these animals brought to bay and fighting for its life, when the reflection forced itself upon me that had it been a buffalo the consequences would have been more serious. We were shooting up the Champa, a small stream flowing into the Brahmini river in Bonai, and forming the southern boundary of the Saranda Forest for some distance. We had done fairly well, having bagged thirteen head of game in a week. Nearing the Koenjure frontier we came on to some grass hills where there were numerous tracks of bison. After a little search we managed to hit on one which the trackers told us was that of a solitary bull. In spite of the eloquence of the guides, who would have had us go after a herd, promising us much sport, we elected for the solitary bison and made our preparations accordingly. There were

BISON PREPARING TO CHARGE.

[*To face page* 251.

three Sahibs, so we tossed for first shot much to the wonderment of the natives, who thought we were performing some charm to ensure our safety if we came up with the bison. We had no difficulty in following up the trail, which was very distinct in the damp ground; and on nearing a thicket of bamboos, the *shikaree* told us to be prepared, as the bison was in all probability among them, taking his midday rest. We therefore proceeded cautiously, keeping the bamboos well to the windward, R——, a hot-headed Welshman who had won the toss, leading. We had got well within the bamboos and were peering cautiously to the front, when suddenly up sprang a large bison within a few yards to our right rear and went tearing down the hill. R—— let drive at once at the stern of the brute as it was making off, and luckily one of his shots took effect and broke its hind leg below the knee. We now made sure of the beast and followed up rapidly, R—— being a long way in advance. There was a slight spur of the hill on which stood a few rocks, and round this the bison had disappeared. On nearing the rocks we saw R—— stop, put his gun to shoulder, bring it down without firing, feel his pockets and then come scampering back to us. He had no ammunition—it was with the *shikaree*—and he had not re-loaded after firing at the bison. It was now at the rocks and had turned to bay and waited for R—— with lowered head; but why it had not charged, especially when it saw its enemy retreating, it is hard to say. Had it been a buffalo R——'s life would not have been worth a minute's purchase.

We now hurried up, and, yes! sure enough, there was the bison ready to receive us. He looked a truly magnificent brute, with his forehead covered with long hair of a bright brown colour, the rest of the head and body being black. The extreme height of the fore-quarters and their massive build make the bison appear a more formidable beast than he is. From his position it was hard to get at a vital spot, and although hats, stones and turbans were thrown near him to induce him to charge, he would not move from his position. Several shots were tried at his head, but made no impression, as we had nothing beyond four drachms of powder in our cartridges, and this did not give sufficient penetration. At last, one of us was compelled to go above the rocks and fire down on him. A shot in the spine near the shoulder did for him.

WILD DUCK TRAPPING IN SOUTH INDIA.

I WAS spending a few days with my friend, Abdul Gunnee, the Commissariat contractor, at his country house in a village not far from Vellore, in the Madras Presidency. My friend's residence was once a palace belonging to one of the magnates of Mahomed Ali's Court when that unscrupulous ruler was Nawab of Arcot. The country around Vellore and Arcot is dotted with many such buildings, erected by the nobles of the Carnatic Court when that State was the chief of the Mahomedan Kingdoms of South India. Surrounded with gardens of cocoanut and areca palms, orange groves, mango, pomegranate and other fruit trees, these old buildings at once testify to the wealth, good taste and love of ease of their former owners.

I had ridden my friend's horses, had admired the fountains which threw their myriad jets in various parts of the garden, had tasted his *mulgovas* and *dil-pusund* (varieties of graft-mango), and now what else was there to do? There was no *shikar* in the neighbourhood beyond duck, and "surely the Sahib was tired of walking in the mud and getting wet to the middle in search of duck that he could buy for a few pice." This was my friend's idea of duck-shooting and all its attendant pleasures. Would I like to see how duck were trapped by the natives? Of course I would, so the village *thaliarree* (watchman) was sent for, and directed to engage some *bestars* (fisherman) to show the Sahib some wild-duck trapping.

There were numerous large tanks in the neighbourhood, which served to irrigate the extensive rice-fields for which this district is famous, and these tanks were the resort of numerous flocks of wild duck at certain seasons of the year. The *bestars* are expert fishermen and takers of water-fowl of all kinds, and have several very ingenious methods of trapping ducks. These birds generally frequent the shallow water near the margin of tanks, as here aquatic plants are most abundant, and among them they find the small shell-fish and fry of fish on which they live. Having sighted a flock of wild duck the *bestar* gets a large earthen pot such as natives use for carrying water. The mouth of the pot must be sufficiently large to admit his head, and in the sides of the pot he knocks two little holes to see out of. Inserting his head into the pot until the rim rests on his shoulders, he wades into the water neck-deep, or crouches down until only the pot is seen above water. The little holes in the sides admit fresh air, and permit him to see. In this fashion he gently moves along in the direction of the flock of ducks. In order to accustom the ducks to the appearance of the pot, several pots mouth down have been previously placed among the weeds the birds are known to frequent, and near to these pots small rafts of plantain bark are placed, with a little paddy, or snails or other bait to attract the birds. The ducks do not take alarm at the approach of the pot under which the *bestar* is concealed, as they imagine it similar to the pots around them. When the *bestar* gets near to the flock he adroitly puts his hand under the nearest duck, seizes it by the legs, and sharply draws it under water. This creates no alarm, as ducks frequently dive down after small fish, etc. He breaks the neck of the duck under water and hangs it to a string round his waist, and then goes for another. In this way he is able to secure a number before the others take alarm and seek safety in flight.

Another method by which large numbers of wild duck are taken alive shows that the natives are keen observers of the habits of the game. A rough model of the body of a duck is made of pith (the substance of which *sola topees* are made), and this is stuck over with the feathers of a wild drake of the species they wish to capture. The feathers are most carefully inserted in the pith so as to give a good imitation of the live bird as it floats on the water. Water fowl do not sleep on the water as is generally believed, but make for an island or the sedge-covered margin of the tank at dusk, and sleep there at night. The *bestars* note the spots the flocks usually resort to at night, and during the absence of the birds in the day they clear away a funnel-shaped entrance in the sedges. The taper end of the funnel, or V, is towards the shore. The whole of the cleared space is covered by a net hung about two feet above the water. In the evening the decoy is floated in the water a little distance away from the trap and a thin string is attached to it, the other end being in the hands of the *bestar*, who is carefully concealed among some bushes or other shelter on the bank. On the approach of the flock at dusk the decoy is made to bob about in a most odd manner. This attracts the wild duck which swim up to know what is wrong with one of their number, as they imagine the decoy to be. The bobbing stops on the near approach of the wild birds, and the decoy swims off in the direction of the trap, being drawn that way by the string in the hands of the *bestar*. Soon the flock follows, and are gradually led into the funnel. When the flock is well within the trap, the net at the mouth is dropped, and the birds secured.

I did not on this occasion see the decoy used and the wild duck captured alive, but I saw the *bestar* at work with the pots. A singular incident occurred while the *bestar* was among the flock of wild ducks. He had drawn down several when suddenly we saw the pot turn over and a great splashing ensue in the water. The ducks took to flight while the *bestar* kept shouting that a *mugger* had seized him by the leg and was drawing him into the water. Fancying there might be some truth in his assertion, as crocodiles had been known to stray away from the trench round the Vellore Fort, where these creatures were to be seen in large numbers (being probably put there in the first instance as one of the means of preventing an enemy entering the fort), we rushed towards the spot, shouting and making as much noise as possible to frighten off the horrid creature. By the time we got round to where the *bestar* had been at work, he came floundering out, yelling and crying out, "*Uppa! Uppa!* (Father! Father!) I am dead!" We noticed some creature, long and black, with white under its stomach, flopping about his waist, which, on nearer approach, we saw was an enormous murrel or ball fish (the Indian trout), common in all South Indian tanks. This is the most voracious of Indian fish and answers in this respect to the pike in England. It had probably made a dash at the wild duck dangling from the waist of the *bestar*, and its gills got entangled in the folds of the cloth he had round his loins. In its efforts to get away it struck frequently against the man's naked thigh, hence his idea that he had been seized by a *mugger*. The fish was fully two and a half feet long and weighed twelve pounds. We congratulated the *bestar* on having caught the mugger instead of being caught by it, and rewarded him for his trouble.

I expressed a wish to my friend to do a little duck shooting on my own account, and he at once directed the *bestars* to make a raft on which I was to seat myself and be towed out by the swimming *bestars*, to any position I wished to make. Four large earthen pots were arranged in the form of a square, and kept in position by means of bamboo framework. Over this a native *charpoy* (bedstead) was placed, and on this I was seated with my heavy duck gun, the *bestars* pushing this fragile yet buoyant concern into deep water. The party on the shore directed our movements, and soon I was ensconced behind some tall rushes near to where several flocks of wild duck were feeding. My *bestars* now left me to drive the duck in my direction, as I hoped to take them on the wing. Soon I heard a quack! as the birds took the wing, and presently a large flock were sailing overhead. Rising on my fragile support to get a better shot, I let drive right and left among them, and then found myself head over heels in the water and nearly drowned. With great difficulty I managed to get back to my seat on the raft, leaving my gun in the water for the *bestars* to recover. In my anxiety to get a good shot at the duck I had stepped too near the edge of the raft, and that, with the heavy recoil of the duck gun, sent one side of the raft down and me into the water. My friend was too much of a gentleman to laugh at my woe-begone figure, wet and covered with mud, but he remarked: "You Sahibs are hard to understand; you will risk your necks to drive a spear into a pig; you will slave all day for birds that can be bought for two pice."

DO TIGERS DREAD FIRE?

It is a popular belief that all wild animals dread fire; hence it is that when camping in the open, in districts frequented by the great carnivora, hunters and travellers kindle large fires round their camps at night to frighten off wild beasts. Livingstone and other writers on African travel have recorded instances where men and domestic animals have been carried away from camp-fires by lions. I have known an instance where a tiger has come night after night and warmed itself at a large fire, not taking the least notice of the coolies working around. We were sinking a prospecting shaft in Chota Nagpore, and as we wished to push the job to completion we worked night and day, in shifts of eight hours. We had no pumps, and as the ground was wet a pulley was fixed over the shaft and sixteen women worked up and down a ramp, pulling a large bucket which was emptied by a man stationed at the mouth of the shaft. The nights in December and January are very cold, and as the hauling was not continuous we kept a large fire going near the shaft to light up the work, round which the women warmed themselves when not working the rope. One night, just after the women had left the fire and gone to the rope, a large tiger was seen to walk deliberately up to the fire, look about for a little while and then lie down and warm itself. Of course there was a stampede of the workpeople at the surface, and the miner in charge of the night-shift was informed of the occurrence. He went to the shaft accompanied by several men, and there saw the tiger lying by the fire. The men shouted and the tiger got up and walked quietly off among the neighbouring bushes. I was told of the circumstance next day but was not inclined to credit it; however, I lent my gun to the night-shift man, and told him not to fire at the tiger if it came again but merely to shout and discharge the gun in the air to scare the beast. The tiger did not turn up next night, nor for several following nights, but it did turn up at irregular intervals, and in time the coolies got used to its coming and would go on with their work as usual. This tiger was well known to the inhabitants of several villages around, and one man claimed relationship with it. He seriously told me it was his great-uncle, who was the *gowala* (cattle herd) of the Tentudee village some years ago. In his time tigers were common in those parts, and carried away numbers of cattle and occasionally human beings. So great was the loss of cattle that the villagers stopped the usual allowance of paddy given to the village herdsman, as they said he was careless and allowed the cattle to stray, so that tigers could easily seize them. His great-uncle was nearly starved by this stoppage of his allowance, and he vowed a vow to Mahadev that if she took the tiger away she could do with him what she pleased. Shortly after the *gowala* died, and since that time the present tiger kept guard over the villages and allowed no other tiger near. When I pointed out that this tiger had killed several buffaloes and cows to my knowledge he replied, "Well, must he not live? Is he to die of hunger? He does not kill men nor allow other tigers here—he is my great-uncle."

The following incident, related by a gentleman of whose veracity there can be no question, would seem to prove that tigers, like the African lion, have occasionally taken away men from the camp-fire and shown no particular dread of light:—

"We were surveying a district lately acquired by the British in North Burmah, and as we had found great difficulty in procuring local labour in the previous season, we took with us from Bangalore a number of Madrassee lascars. The country was in a very disturbed state, as bands of dacoits looted villages and robbed and murdered travellers wherever they found them. Six military police under a *naik* were sent with us for our protection, and a couple of elephants to carry our baggage and provisions, as nothing was to be had in the district we were going into. The first part of our journey lay through low marshy country, with here and there a little rice cultivation, but we soon got past this into a 'terai' at the foot of a range of hills, and here our troubles began. The country was the most difficult for survey operations that I have seen. Dense jungle and tall grass with fearful canes everywhere. You could take a sight nowhere. Lines had to be cleared before we could make any progress. We had scarcely cleared a mile or two of pathway, when we missed one of our Madrassees. He was not missed till we got home in the evening. Fancying he might have strayed away and got lost in the jungle, we kindled large fires, kept shouting out at intervals, and I got the police to fire off an occasional shot, thinking that if he were within hearing this might direct him to our camp. Next day search-parties were organised and the country carefully scoured, but the men would not go far for fear of losing themselves, the jungle being so dense. After a two days' wait and continuous search we were obliged to go on with our work, having reported the circumstance to head-quarters. On the fourth day after the disappearance of the man, a second Madrassee was missing. We had a suspicion that the first man had deserted, but in this instance that could not be, as we were too far advanced into the heart of the jungle for the man to find his way back alone. It could not be dacoits, as they would not molest a coolie with nothing valuable about him, and as we were well out of the Wa country, that being on the other side of the river, the head-hunters were not to be feared. The general opinion was that this man had also strayed away into the forest and had become lost; he might find his way to some Shan settlement on the hills, or stray back to the open ground near the river. The men received orders to keep as much as possible together, and even when going into the forest for water or other purposes to go two at a time. In another four days we had made about fifteen miles, when a third man was missing at night. The men used to cluster round the camp-fires at night; a policeman was on guard at intervals of four hours, and the elephants were picketed near at hand; yet none knew how the man had disappeared. The police on guard said that at about midnight one of the coolies left the fire to go into the bushes for a little while. He thought he saw the man return, but he was not sure. A careful search was made all around, yet no trace of the man was visible, nor track of any wild animal. A great fear fell on all. I confess that I myself felt some alarm at this unknown danger. If we knew the source from which to look for an attack, a proper defence might be provided. But here were three men missing, at intervals of four days, and none could say how or where they had gone. Was it a head-hunting party of the wild Wa that had crossed the river and were carrying off human heads to grace the village 'Avenue of great deeds'? Was it a party of dacoits that were following us up and not feeling strong enough to attack us together were cutting off stragglers and would eventually storm the camp. It could not be a tiger for there were no signs of these creatures about, and then what of the intervals of four days, and the following up of our camp, which had shifted quarters some thirty miles since the first man was missing?

"The men were unmanageable from fear. They would not leave camp but in groups of half a dozen, and when the fatal fourth day came round again, not a soul would leave the clearing to bring even a pot of water. That night extra precautions were used; additional fires were kindled all round the camp, and the elephants were made to patrol round and round while darkness lasted. The morning-roll was called and thank Heaven! not a soul was missing. Having got over the fatal day, the men took heart and said we could go on working for the next three days, but on the fourth the same precautions were to be taken. We shifted camp a few miles and did an indifferent day's work, the men going about cautiously and in groups. That night an enormous fire was kindled a little distance from the entrance of my tent, and in a circle round the large fire, and at some distance from it, smaller fires were burned, the men sleeping within this circle of fire. The night passed off without disturbance, and we were congratulating ourselves on having at last overcome the danger, when the roll was called and a Madrassee was reported missing. The men who slept on either side of him were questioned. No, he had not left the camp fire, at least not to their knowledge; they had not missed him in the morning. While this examination was going on, an exclamation from Kissen Sing, the *naik* of the military police, drew us to the spot where the missing man had slept at the large fire. Motioning the crowd to keep off, the *naik* called me to the place, and there pointed out what appeared to be a drop of blood, and, what was of more significance still, the well-marked pug of a tiger. The marks were so small that I said these were those of a panther, but Kissen Sing, who was a noted *shikaree*, and had often taken part in tiger shooting expeditions in Tirhoot, declared it was a tigress and with cubs. How on earth he inferred all this I cannot make out, but subsequent events proved he was right. He was of opinion that the tigress was answerable for the four persons missing. She had followed us up from day to day and when pressed with hunger had carried off one of the men. Now that we knew the source of danger, the men were not so much scared, although still timid and moving about in groups. A careful search was made with the aid of the elephants, but not a trace of the tiger or its prey could be found. We shifted camp that day and the next and took no extra precautions, as Kissen Sing said the tiger would not look for a victim till it was again hungry. On the third night he had a strong platform erected, about twelve feet from the ground, among the trees, and upon this the men slept, the elephants being chained one on each side. The men slept in safety, and there were no casualties to report in the morning. The next day the same precautions were taken, and the men safely stowed on the platform before it was dark. I had called for dinner, and Ramaswamy, my Madrassee cook, had just left the kitchen *pal* (small tent) to dish the dinner on a camp-table outside, on which there was a kerosene lantern. The man and the table were not ten yards from me, and I was seated in my hill tent directly facing him, when I saw something dark spring over the table, seize the cook by the neck, and spring back. Not a sound from the cook—not a rustle of the leaves—nothing disturbed. The cook's mate within the *pal* heard nothing, and here was the cook carried away from within a few feet of a bright light. I immediately raised the alarm, and fired off a couple of shots in the direction the tiger had taken, and the police began a regular fusillade. Next morning a careful search was made, but to no purpose. The men declined to work further, and said they would leave me and go back in a body. They did not care for their back wages; their lives were of more consequence. I was without a cook, so there was nothing for it but the back track. The elephants were loaded and back we went. We had almost reached our last camp when the elephants stopped, and sounded the alarm by striking the ground with their trunks, making a kind of kettle-drum sound. Kissen Sing said there was a tiger about. We proceeded cautiously, the men keeping near to the elephants. On getting into our former camp, and near to the watch-fire, there we saw the head and other portions of my cook Ramaswamy. The tigress and two cubs were evidently disturbed at their meal, as we saw their pug marks in close proximity to the remains of the cook, which were on the ashes of our camp fire. We gave the remains of the poor fellow what burial we could and hurried off on our return journey. We passed several other of our late camps and did fifteen miles that day. The next day we had passed one camp and were just entering a second when the elephants swerved on one side of what was the site of our camp fire, and here on the ashes we found the skull, feet, and thigh bones of a second human being, which, from scraps of cloth about, were recognised as those of the Madrassee carried off a few days before Ramaswamy, the cook. The next day the remains of another lascar were come on, several camps away. We could now see the cunning tactics of the tigress by which she had avoided detection. She had actually followed us up on our own tracks, and, having made a kill, dragged the unfortunate back to our previous day's camp, some four or five miles off, and there stayed with her cubs till pressed by hunger to follow us up again. The marks of the elephants and men made a kind of a beaten track, along which she would leave no trace. The cubs, which Kissen Sing said were not more than six months old, judging from their pugs, were not allowed to accompany their mother when on the hunt, but remained behind to feast on what she brought. We hurried back to head-quarters and saw nothing of tigress or cubs. The survey in that locality had to be abandoned that season, as none of the lascars would work there."

A CHAT WITH A SNAKE-CHARMER.

"WILL the Huzoor see the snakes? Many snakes; snakes from Raipore, Bilaspore; snakes from the hills, and snakes from the plains; snakes of all kinds. Yes, the Sahib is right; we are humbugs. I am a poor man, and I must talk for my stomach. I have *nags* (cobras), and I have *kraits*. I have the swift *dhamna* (whip snake), and I have the deadly, yet tiny, *bingraj* (the sand viper, the most deadly of all snakes). No, Sahib, I have not the *raj nag* (king-cobra), nor have I got the *bandpost*. I see the Huzoor understands about snakes, since he asks for the rarest of all snakes, the *raj nag* and the *bandpost*. I have seen the *raj nag*, but I have never had one myself. They are useless for our purposes, as they are too fierce and cannot be tamed. The *bandpost* also is hard to keep, as it lives on bees, and where am I to get bees all the year round? Yes, the Huzoor is right; the *bandpost* stings with its tail and bites with its mouth, and both are deadly. Have I seen it sting anything?—Yes, I have seen it sting a dog that went near to smell it after its head had been broken, and the dog died. The Huzoor does not

SNAKE CHARMERS.

[*To face page* 268.

believe me? The Huzoor is right, I am a liar, and the Huzoor is my father and my mother; but the *bandpost* has got a sting in its tail, like a scorpion. Am I not a catcher of snakes and should I not know?

"Yes, I can cure the bite of all snakes—all but the *bingraj*. It is the smallest of snakes, and yet if it bites, death is almost instantaneous. It is generally found during the hot months in the fine dust of pathways. It lives in the dust, and feeds on insects, ant-lions and such like. See, here it is"—and he turned out a tiny snake about six inches long from a purse he had stuck in his waist-cloth. The creature looked somewhat like a dry twig, and was very slow in its movements, and but for the forked tongue which it protruded from its mouth now and again it gave no sign of life. Its flat viper head showed that it belonged to the poisonous family of snakes. I had often heard from the natives of this deadly snake, but this was the first I had ever seen. It is commoner in the Punjab and Rajpootana than in the more wooded districts of India, and is well known for its deadly venom. The natives say that if this snake bites one in the foot, death is instantaneous; but if it bites one in the chest, a gentle drowsy sensation of sleep overcomes one, and one dies with a pleasant look on the face. Rajpoot women when they wish to commit suicide apply one of these snakes to the bosom and make it bite them there, when they enjoy the most pleasurable sensations and die quietly. There is no cure ; whether it bites in the foot or chest, death comes all the same, only the one is quicker than the other. Can there be any connection between this story and that of Cleopatra and the viper ?

"Yes, Sahib, I can cure the bite of the cobra and *krait*, in fact, of all serpents but the *bingraj*. I can show the Sahib the medicines I use if he will give me *bucksheesh* (a present). This is *nag ka thitha* (gall of a cobra). If this is applied to the bite at once there is no danger of death, although the person bitten will have fainting fits and cold sweats for a week ; but we give a little gall mixed in milk to the person once a day, and he is cured. I am proof against snake venom, as I take a little snake poison every week, in a pill. I have taken it for years. All our people take snake poison, and we are not afraid of snakes. We dip a paddy-straw into snake venom and wipe the straw on a paste of *hillul* (a creeping plant that looks like sarsaparilla), and this we swallow. We must take this every week, or it will have no effect. I have been bitten frequently on the back of my hands by snakes that I keep. Yes, we draw the venom-fangs, but they grow again in a fortnight or a month. We can also take out the venom without drawing the fangs. See, Sahib, if I press here, in the snake's jaw, with this piece of stick, the fangs are erected and the poison exudes at the point of the fang. The fangs are hollow like a pipe, and the poison comes out through this pipe when the poison bags are squeezed. We sell the poison to the *baghmarees* (tiger killers) and *kobirajs* (native physicians).

"Will the Sahib now see the snakes dance, since he has talked his stomach full, or will I catch the snakes that are in the Sahib's bungalow?"

I was residing in a thatched bungalow that had been uninhabited for years, and the old straw in the roof seemed to be a breeding place for snakes. I was seated in the verandah one evening just after a shower of rain, reading the newspaper, when something dropped on to my lap. To my horror I saw it was a small snake of the viper or house *krait* kind. In a moment I was up, tossing the snake on the floor, and crushed it under foot. I resumed my reading, but in about a quarter of an hour I heard a flop on the floor just behind my chair, and on looking round saw this was another snake of the same size and kind as that I had just killed. This I despatched with a stick, and, feeling that I could no longer enjoy my reading when there was a chance of a deadly serpent dropping on to me, I went into the bedroom, the roof of which had a ceiling of cloth. I had been in the bedroom about an hour when I noticed a snake, similar in all respects to the other two, creeping in at the door. It was now patent that a brood of these creatures must have been hatched somewhere in the roof, and were now on the move. A careful search was made, and the doors secured for the night. In the morning my servant killed a fourth snake in the verandah. In all we killed some fourteen snakes in the bungalow in three months, all of them poisonous.

I thought perhaps the snake-charmer had heard of this plague of snakes, and wished to take advantage of it for his own purposes. No, I did not want a *krait* from the bungalow, but would he bring a snake of a different kind from the bed of *zinnias* in front of the bungalow? Yes, he was quite prepared to bring a snake from anywhere, even out of the floor of the verandah. Fearing a trick, I made him divest himself of as much clothing as possible, and with only his calabash snake-charming pipes to his mouth he approached the *zinnias* in a cautious manner, myself and my servants watching his every movement closely. He kept blowing vigorously, and circled round the bed of *zinnias* once or twice, and then with a leap he was into the flower-bed, and hauled forth a large snake about six feet long which struggled violently to get away. But he held it firmly by the middle and brought it to the verandah, when there was a stampede among the lookers-on, myself among the number. We made him put away his capture in one of his snake baskets before we again approached.

Suspecting that he had put one of his tame snakes in the flower-bed beforehand, in case I should ask him to catch a snake, I now determined to watch him more closely and to give him no chance of preparation. I said, "I will give you five rupees if you will take a cobra out of there"—pointing to a spot in the cement floor about four

A SNAKE FROM THE ZINNIA BED.

[*To face page* 272

feet away from where I was sitting. The snake-charmer readily consented, and began a kind of a war-dance in the verandah, keeping step to a weird tune he played on his calabash. The only stitch of cloth he had on was a rag, some six inches wide between his legs, fastened before and behind to a cord round his waist, so that it was impossible for him to conceal anything in his clothing. I asked my servants to watch him closely, while I did the same. After dancing a measure or two, and approaching and receding several times from the spot I indicated, he suddenly shouted "There! Sahib, there!" pointing to the spot. All eyes were involuntarily turned thither, and he leaped forward and pretended to clutch something from the ground, and held up a cobra about two and a half feet long. There were shouts of approbation and wonder from my servants in which I did not join. It is a common trick among conjurors of all nations when some sleight of hand is to be performed to call off attention from the expert's hands to some other spot. I was prepared for this, so did not look at the spot the snake-charmer pointed to, but kept my eyes on him, watching his every movement. As he sprang forward to seize the supposed snake, as quick as lightning one hand was thrust into his hair, which was tied in a large knot somewhat like that the Cingalese women wear, and from this hiding place he drew the small cobra he pretended to pick off the floor.

The man quickly noticed that I did not join

in the plaudits of his audience and said: "Who can deceive the Sahibs? we are their children, and we learn from them. It is for my stomach's sake, Huzoor, but don't you tell the fools around. The Sahib will give me what he pleases since I have not earned the five rupees."

THE HUNTING LEOPARD OR CHEETAH.

It is singular that while the tiger, the leopard and the wolf are the recognised enemies of the cultivator, in that they prey on his flocks and herds, and that the Government offers a reward for the destruction of these predatory animals, probably the most daring and destructive of all, and the one which does more damage to cattle and goats than all the other wild animals put together, is generally regarded as a harmless creature and one to be protected rather than destroyed. One reason perhaps for this good name is that the cheetah, or hunting leopard, has never been known to prey on mankind, while tigers, leopards and wolves are all known to be man-eaters on occasion. The cheetah also can be domesticated and taught to run down antelope and small deer, and thus be rendered subservient to man—another reason for overlooking its well-known habit of preying on the sheep, goats and calves of the villagers. But for courage, daring, cunning and audacity it can give points to any beast of the field, and it is fortunate indeed that it does not prey on man, as few would be safe from its attacks.

At Jeraikela, on the Bengal-Nagpur Railway, a villager had a pet spotted deer, which would follow him about like a dog. I frequently wished to purchase it, and offered him a price many times its value and sufficient to tempt most natives. But he would not sell. He was as fond of the deer as the deer was of him. His hut was in the heart of the village. One warm moonlight night he drew his *charpoy* (bedstead) as usual across the entrance of his hut and slept on it. While he was asleep, a hunting leopard crept under his charpoy, seized and killed the deer, and crept back the way it came, drawing the deer after it, and made off to the woods. The man only knew of his loss on awakening in the morning, when the unmistakable dog-like foot-prints of the animal showed who the midnight marauder was. Not long ago one of these brutes entered the village of Bendee during the dark hours just before dawn. It dug a passage for itself through the wattle-and-dab walls of the bazaar-man's hut, seized and killed a two-year-old calf, and endeavoured to drag the body through the passage it had made for itself, but the calf's body was too large to pass that way. The noise made by the cheetah's efforts to drag the calf through the hole in the wall awakened an old woman who was sleeping in the hut, and she immediately opened the door, rushed out and raised an outcry. The cheetah, seeing the door open, re-entered the dwelling and pulled the calf away through the door! It made off to a neighbouring nullah and there devoured the stomach and a great part of the rump. The calf certainly weighed over 200 lbs.; yet the cheetah was able to drag the body several hundred yards, when its own weight could not have been over 70 lbs. even if full grown.

The cheetah is particularly fond of dog's flesh and does useful service in carrying off superfluous pariah dogs which otherwise would increase to such an extent as to be a source of danger to the villagers themselves. It is seldom one sees a dog in the country where the hunting leopard has taken up its abode. Sooner or later even the 'cutest of 'cute pariah dogs falls a victim to its arch enemy. I have had seven dogs carried away from my bungalow in eighteen months. Among these was a black pariah that the servants had named *Hooseearee* (the wary one), so alert was it. It would never on any pretence leave the servants' quarters after nightfall. I often tried to tempt it out with a bone after dinner, but no; hungry or not, Hooseearee was not to be cajoled into the open. One night while I was having my dinner, a *pheeall* (an animal of the jackal kind said to act as a decoy to tigers, leopards and other of the great carnivora) sent forth its hideous howl near the servants' quarters. I was long anxious to secure one of these creatures, as I had heard so much of them, but had never come across anyone who had shot one. I ran for my Winchester and hurriedly loading it went into the verandah facing the servants' quarters. The moon was slightly obscured with clouds, so that objects in the open could be seen, but not very distinctly. Hooseearee was barking loudly, when again the unearthly yell of the *pheeall* was heard, this time just in front of the servants' quarters. This was too much for flesh and blood, and Hooseearee gave chase. Instead of making for the jungle, which was near at hand, the *pheeall* made for some logs of timber lying in the open. As soon as the black dog in pursuit of the *pheeall* neared the timber, swift as a flash of light the cheetah was on him and seized him by the back of the neck; a single bark of agony and Hooseearee was no more. I fired twice at the cheetah, but he was off like a bird, carrying the body of the dog with him. It looked as if it were all planned out by the cheetah and the *pheeall;* the latter was to decoy the dog out, and run in the direction of the logs behind which the cheetah was concealed. I cannot conceive any other reason why the *pheeall* should have run to the logs instead of to the jungle.

After the loss of Hooseearee I had all my dogs shut up in a godown at dusk every evening. On several occasion I was awakened by the furious barking of the dogs, and generally found signs in the morning that the cheetah had tried to enter through a barred window. After several attempts to break in this way he gave it up, as he found iron bars too hard for even his powerful teeth. But one day three of my dogs accompanied the syces taking out my horses for their morning constitutional. All three were large dogs, half-breeds, about the size of a foxhound. One of them was particularly large and heavy. All had broad leather collars with steel pricks to protect the neck from the assaults of wild animals. The horses were being promenaded along the road within half-a-mile of my bungalow, when a cheetah sprang out of the neighbouring bushes and seized the largest of the dogs by the neck, in spite of his protecting collar, and made off with him

The cheetah is said to be the swiftest animal under the sun for distances not exceeding half-a-mile. In six hundred yards he could probably give a fleet greyhound half the distance and overtake him. The cheetah, or hunting leopard, in no way resembles the ordinary leopard or panther. The latter has retractile claws like the cat, while the cheetah's paws are like those of the dog. Most *shikarees* are agreed that he belongs to the hyæna family, and is to that animal what the greyhound is to the foxhound. Sir Samuel Baker has stated that he has seen one of these creatures run up the smooth trunk of a tree for about fifteen feet and then crouch in the fork, out of reach of its keepers, whence it could only be tempted down by the offer of a ladleful of warm blood taken from an antelope just slain by another hunting leopard used in the morning's chase. It is generally believed that the cheetah is only found in the more open parts of the scrub jungle of Central India, but I have killed them in the dense forest of Saranda in Chota Nagpur. The skin is differently marked to that of the panther. Both have a yellowish brown ground with black spots. The spots on the panther are rosettes; on the cheetah they are simply black dabs without a central opening of yellow. For purposes of hunting the antelope and other small deer the cheetah must be caught when full grown and then domesticated. When taken as cubs they never learn to hunt.

THE BANDYPORE MAN-EATER.

It was before the days of railways when the Seegor pass *viâ* Mysore was the only road to Ootacamund, and bullock transits the quickest means of travelling. It was a fair road from Bangalore to Mysore, but from thence onwards to Seegor at the foot of the Neilgherries there was nothing but a clayey track (known as a second class road) with quagmires and pits during the rainy season, in which it was a miracle if your coach wheel did not stick and remain a fixture till help was procured from Bandypore or Mussencoil, the only large villages along this route. Such had been my fate the previous July, when travelling to Madras from Ooty *viâ* Bangalore. My transit came to grief in a mud-hole in the centre of the road and in our efforts to extract the wheel by means of a long pole used as a lever, a felloe was smashed. This necessitated a delay of two days at the Bandypore bungalow, before a new felloe could be made by the village artizan, and it was while thus stranded far away from the haunts of civilization that I first heard of the Bandypore man-eater. Having nothing better to do I had strolled into the village to watch the carpenter at his work, and help with advice as to the repairs of the transit, and was soon in friendly converse with the villagers who crowded round the "Doray" (gentleman). "Had the Daveru heard of the '*pille*' (tiger) '*perun pillee*' (large tiger) which was living on them and on their children, and their cattle? *Poojah* (propitiatory ceremonies) was of no avail; the devil of a tiger had even carried away the *poojahree* (village priest), and now, no one was safe; they could not go to the jungle for firewood, and *brattees* were consequently getting dear. Would the Doray stay a day and try and shoot the brute; his children (the motley assemblage around) would be grateful for ever."

The Doray had nothing better than a six-shooter —a kind of travelling companion—with which to try conclusions with the monster if met with, and as he did not like to add himself to the already long list of those the brute had killed and eaten, he, with many expressions of what he *would* do if he had the weapons, gratefully declined the offers of those who volunteered to lead him to the edge of the forest the tiger haunted, and leave him there. On my return journey to Ooty some eight months after, I again found myself delayed at Bandypore, and this time because the transit drivers refused to drive through the Tippoo Kadu as that portion of the forest was called, as two transit drivers had been carried off from their coaches only a few days before by the man-eating tiger.

At the bungalow I found Messrs. Kaye and Ward, the Government Tiger Slayers. Kaye I

A MAN-EATING TIGER.

[*To face page* 283

frequently met later on as a successful coffee planter on the Hills, and a better shot or a more fearless hunter I have never seen. Ward belonged to the 60th Rifles, then stationed at Ootacamund, and had been specially selected for his keen *shikar* instincts to exterminate the tigers which then infested the Neilgherries. I have lost sight of him for many years, but I am told that he left the army and joined the Madras Railway where he did right good work. He had so happy a way of relating his *shikar* experiences—so little of the *ego* in them, yet so full of dash—that the long evenings seemed to fly while listening to deeds of daring unrecorded in printer's ink. If ever he writes his experiences of jungle life, his will be a book worth reading. Kaye and Ward had heard of the Bandypore man-eater and were now collecting information on the spot, and finding out its favourite haunts. They had already been out a couple of days but had not succeeded in coming across it, and had only heard that morning that a coolie on the Moyar Coffee Estate, some fifteen miles away, had been carried off the previous day by the brute, and they were now hurrying to get off while the scent was warm. I had a new Westley-Richards with me, a recent purchase in Madras, and was anxious to try its qualities on big game, but the time at my disposal was not enough to permit of my joining them. In such company I believe I would have faced a dozen tigers, as both were deadly shots, and as cool as cool could be under the most exciting circumstances. Wishing them all success I saw them off and then went on to the village to induce the transit drivers to supply bullocks for the next two stages, there being none available at the station five miles off, the men having deserted owing to fear of the tiger. I pointed out to the men that with two such noted *shikarees* as Kaye and Ward before us there was nothing to fear as they were certain to account for the tiger if it was about. After much persuasion I managed to procure two drivers and two sets of bullocks, one to yoke to the coach and the other to follow behind, to drag from the next station. It was about four in the afternoon when we set out, my servant on the box beside the driver, and the extra pair of bullocks trotting close behind the keeper at their heels urging them on. To inspire confidence I had my double Westley-Richards in my hand, having carefully loaded it with an extra charge of powder, ready for contingencies. Keeping a bright look-out ahead, we were jogging along in the hot sun and amid clouds of dust, and hoped to get to the changing station in a few minutes. I had been chaffing the driver as to the man-eater, and asked him where it had got to ? Was he alarmed now ; and had he not done wisely in coming with me ; when suddenly with a snort of alarm the bullocks behind the transit galloped to the front and went tearing along with tails erect. Turning to learn what had alarmed them, I saw an enormous brute of a tiger slouching off in the brushwood beside the road, with the unfortunate bullock driver in its mouth! It held him by the neck and his legs were dragging on the ground as it was stealing off. I rapidly cocked my rifle, and placing the stock to my shoulder took a rough aim and pulled off both triggers, as I hoped that even if I missed the tiger, the sudden report would make him drop his victim. Snap! snap! went both barrels, and I found I had not capped the gun (this was in the days before breech-loaders were in common use). By this time the bullocks yoked to the transit had also taken the alarm and were dashing away after their companions and no amount of tugging at the reins would stop them in their wild flight. It was fully a mile before they could be brought under control and then no amount of persuasion or threats would induce either my servant or the driver to go back with me to try and recover the body of the poor fellow carried off by the man-eater. That he was dead there could be no doubt, as his neck must have been broken by the first bite of those tremendous jaws. Probably the brute would have begun his gruesome meal ere this, but still there was a chance of recovering some portion of his body. The next best thing to be done was to hurry on and try and overtake Messrs. Kaye and Ward and bring them back to the scene of this dreadful adventure. I felt that I had indirectly been the cause of the man's death, as it was my representation that had induced him to come with me. We hurried on till we came to a small hamlet on the southern skirts of the forest, the inhabitants of which had securely fastened their doors at dusk, as this tiger had been known to enter a village and carry off a woman who was drawing water from a well. We learned from the villagers that the Government tiger slayers had left the road and taken a short cross cut to Moyar. While in converse with the villagers a transit from Ooty drew up, and in it were two officers of the 60th Rifles on their way to Bandypore to look up the famous tiger. My tale was soon told, and after a hasty meal we set out for the spot where the driver was carried off. We had to do the driving ourselves as the natives were too frightened to sit on the box alone. We camped at the deserted transit station and were out betimes next morning, but nothing could be found of the body, nor were there any traces of the tiger. We searched all that day and part of the next, but no tiger, nor any signs of the unfortunate man's body could we see. Leaving the officers to continue the hunt the transit was once more turned to the Ooty direction, I driving, and my servant inside—(the driver had decamped the previous day). I was in hopes of getting a change of bullocks and new driver at Seegor, and was driving along slowly when we arrived at a large stream (the Moyar river) about two in the afternoon. My servant asked me to stop a little as he wished to obtain a drink at the river. There is a fine masonry bridge of several arches over the stream, and on this I stopped the coach to allow my boy to quench his thirst. He had barely been away a minute when he came hurrying back, and in a trembling voice told me the tiger was in the river with all his body in the water, and merely his head out. Telling him to hold the bullocks by their nose-strings I got my Westley-Richards, this time careful to see it capped, and stealing to the parapet and peeping over saw, sure enough, the enormous head of a tiger just protruding out of the water. Luckily it was looking in a direction opposite to that from which we had come and the noise of the stream had prevented its hearing our coach-wheels. Taking careful aim at the head I fired, keeping the other barrel ready if I required to use it. With a convulsive movement forward, that brought its body half out of the water, the tiger fell never to rise again, the ball having gone (as I afterwards saw) clean through the brain. Waiting for some time to make sure the beast was not foxing nor merely stunned by the shot, and finding no movement in the body, we unyoked the bullocks and fastened them to a tree, and then went down to examine my kill. It was a magnificent male tiger, one of the largest I have seen, and in splendid condition. There were no marks of mange about the skin to show that it was a man-eater—the popular idea being that eating human flesh causes the tiger to become mangy; this, like many other popular beliefs, is incorrect, as I learned by later experience, some of the finest skins being those of man-eaters. With the greatest difficulty I and my servant were just able to drag the body out of the water, and there I had to leave it till my servant returned with a cart from Seegor. The villagers of Seegor on arrival pronounced the tiger to be the man-eater of Bandypore, but this I was not inclined to credit as I then believed in the mange theory. However, I allowed them to carry the body in triumph to Seegor, where certain ceremonies were performed by the village priest over the dead tiger's body. On careful measurement before skinning, the length from tip of tail to snout was ten feet two inches. After skinning the length was nearly eleven feet. I wrote to the Collector of Coimbatore relating the circumstance of the kill, and some two months later received a letter of thanks and a Government reward of two hundred rupees for having unwittingly shot the man-eater of Bandypore.

STRANGE PETS.

It is unaccountable the taste some men have for odd pets. I knew a man in the Railway at Coopum, in the fifties, who had a rock-snake or boa for a pet. He was an assistant on construction at the time the Madras Railway was being built from Jollarpett to Bangalore, and the snake was taken in a large-sized mouse-trap with a falling door. The snake was known to take shelter in a natural fissure in the rocks that abound on the *ghauts* near Coopum, and the trap was set near its entrance and baited with a live fowl. The snake was found within the trap next morning and the fowl had disappeared, probably down the snake's throat. My friend transferred the snake to a rabbit hutch and there attended to it himself until it got quite tame and allowed him to handle it freely. He would take it out and fold it round his neck like a comforter, or stretch it out at arm's length, when it would wind itself round his arm. Its length when caught was nearly five feet, but it grew very quickly on the diet of eggs and young chickens that it got twice a week, and in six months' time, it was quite six feet and weighed fifty pounds. After a time it was allowed to roam the house at will when its master was within doors, and only caged when he was at work. It appeared to know him well and recognised his voice, as it would protrude its tongue on his approach and raise its head.

There was nothing it more dearly loved than to nestle under the blankets near my friend's chest, in the cold days of December and January. It was a long time before his dogs would take to it, but a little terrier soon made friends and then the others tolerated it all except Fan, a fine spaniel, which could never be persuaded to allow the snake to approach her. There seemed to be reason in this antipathy, for some time after Fan had a litter of four puppies, and one morning when the master was having his breakfast and the boa was loose as usual, Fan left her puppies a moment and went into the breakfast room, on the chance of getting a scrap. Shortly after she set up a tremendous barking, and on going out to see what was the matter, my friend found the boa coiled up in Fan's corner, and two of her puppies missing. The boa was in disgrace for some time after, and not allowed out of its hutch.

Visitors were chary of approaching my friend's house, and always stopped at the gate and shouted out, "Put away your d——d snake" before venturing within doors. Its presence also kept away the natives, and few of the domestic servants would go near it. When carefully fed it was perfectly harmless and slept away the most of its existence. During the time it shed its outer skin it would take no food for about a month, but would constantly rub itself against any rough substance in order to assist in peeling off the exterior gauze-like membrane.

Leopards were common about Coopum and proved a great nuisance, as they carried off a great number of my friend's dogs. One night the little fox-terrier that had first struck up a friendship with the boa was asleep near the steps of the verandah, the snake was coiled up near it, and my friend was in his office-room getting through some correspondence when he heard a sharp "yap!" (the sound a dog emits when seized by the neck by a leopard). He at once recognised the sound and knew that one of his dogs had been seized by a leopard. Rapidly picking up his gun which stood loaded in a corner of the room, he hurried out and heard a tremendous row in the verandah, as if a dozen cats were engaged in deadly strife. In the imperfect light he could see a dark mass wriggling about, and fancying it was the leopard, he fired two shots at it. When lights were fetched, he found "Tricks," the little fox-terrier, quite dead with a dreadful bite on the neck, and a small-sized leopard still in the coils of the boa and nearly dead from the gunshots. With some difficulty the snake was made to uncoil, and it was then found that my friend's shots in the dark had also seriously wounded the snake. It had probably seen the leopard attack the terrier, and had flung itself on the leopard, and would have in all probability squeezed it to death had not my friend unfortunately shot both. It died in the course of the day.

Lieutenant Frere, a son of Sir Bartle Frere, who was well known in Bangalore twenty or thirty years ago, had an enormous tame hyæna. This he picked up when a very tiny cub on the Agram plains one field day, and brought it up on the "bottle" until it was large enough to eat meat, when it shared their food with his dogs. It grew up quite tame and apparently much attached to its master, as it whined sorrowfully whenever he left it. Nothing pleased it better than to accompany him in his walks. It would trot close to his heels, and no amount of barking or baying by dogs would make it leave its position. It made a splendid pet, but for its insufferable odour, which repeated tubbing could not remove. The enormous power of its jaw was amply verified by the way it would crush up and swallow the largest beef-bones. It was thought so tame and harmless that it was left always loose and only chained up when Frere went to parade, to prevent its following him.

One morning he was strolling along the ride on South Parade with the hyæna at his heels when a native *ayah* with a perambulator passed. Without a moment's warning the hyæna sprang at her and tore her cloth, when Frere rushed up and struck it repeatedly with a light walking cane he had with him. The hyæna left the woman and attacked its master furiously, seized him by the forearm, and would have probably done him serious mischief had not Mr. L. been passing that way and seen the attack. He at once rushed up and with a stout stick he had with him, brained the creature.

Snakes and hyænas are strange pets, but strangest of all is a full-grown tiger, and such a pet had Major Mansell-Pleydell. It used to be chained up just in front of the door of his bungalow. The Major had a method of running up bills with local tradesmen, but there was great difficulty in getting payment, as none of the bill collectors were venturesome enough to cross the guardian at the door. It was a great joke of the Major's when asked to pay his bill to reply, " have you sent your bill; your man has never presented it at my house." Brutus, as the tiger was named, seemed to know what was required of him. When chained before his master's door he would lie with his head between his forepaws and watch the gate. If a stranger entered he would lift his head and breathe heavily, and this was enough to scare the most venturesome of bill collectors.

Pleydell and another were out shooting at Arsikeri (before railway times) and Brutus went with them. The scrub jungle making up the Amrut Mahal Kavals, to the south of the village, was a noted place for tiger. The native *shikarees* had marked down four of these dreaded beasts—a tiger and tigress with two well-grown cubs. In the morning's shoot Pleydell had been very successful, and had bagged the mother and two cubs before breakfast, within a mile of the travellers' bungalow. The tiger was still about, and they made up their minds to try and get him before night. Brutus was chained up before leaving. Pleydell and his friend, each with a *shikaree* and beaters, had taken different routes. The friend had been very unsuccessful and was returning to the bungalow in no good humour, when the *skikaree* pointed out a large tiger just off the path, evidently watching something in the distance. It was but a moment's work to bring his rifle to his shoulder and let the tiger have one in the chest; as it bounded forward a second shot fair in the head sent it over quite dead. Rushing forward to view his triumph, he saw Brutus—Pleydell's pet—dead before him!

THE KODERMA MAN-EATER.

" How long, oh *Sahib!* how long are thy servants to be food for the tiger ? Are you not our father and mother, and we, servants of the Great Queen ? Can you not tell the *Dipty Sahib* or the *Lat Sahib*, and proclaim by beat of drum in the three *thanas* of Chorporan, Koderma and Gaya that the *agrarees* (charcoal-burners) are not to be eaten of tigers ? What have we done that we, who share the forests with the wild beasts, who burn charcoal and collect iron-sand for our smelting furnaces in the most lonesome parts of the jungle, should now be debarred from pursuing our daily avocations by this son of *shaitan* (devil). It mattered not when he killed the cheating *golas* (herdsmen), who watered our milk and sold curds that had gone bad ; or even the evil-smelling *chamar* (the lowest caste in the native village, whose perquisite it is to have all cattle killed by tigers, or which have died from disease), who robs the tiger of half his kill, and even eats that which Mahadev has slain. Had I not given Kadun, the Poojaree, two white cocks to be sacrificed at the shrine of the Great Mother, when Bola was taken by the tiger, and then did not we charcoal-burners subscribe and buy a *kassee* (he-goat) when Moortah fell a victim? No later than bazaar-day we got two pigs from Chirala and sacrificed at Kali's shrine, and yet at noon this very day my own mother's sister's son was taken at Bageetand by the devil and son of a devil."

Such was the tale of Jiban—*shikaree* and charcoal-burner—poured out in disjointed phrases on my arrival at camp after a few days' absence.

Many is the fine haunch of venison, plump peafowl and smaller game of sorts that Jiban has supplied for my larder, and many is the chat I have had with him on the habits of wild beasts, with which he is familiar; his days being spent in charcoal-burning and many of his nights in sitting behind a light screen of branches at some forest pool that wild animals frequented. He was a little bit given to exaggeration, but withal truthful; hence it was that I gave more attention to his story of the famous man-eating tiger that was doing so much damage to human life in the police *thanas* of Koderma, Chorporan and Gaya. This brute made his first human kill in March, and since that date no fewer than twenty-seven persons have been carried off in the three above-named police circuits within three months—this is the record even among famous man-eating tigers. Natives say that the number is even higher, and that it is the invariable custom of this ferocious brute to kill and devour a human being every other day, and that many of these cases are not reported to the police.

Bageetand has gained an unenviable reputation, as from here no fewer than four people have been carried off within the last few months. Three *golas* (cattle herdsmen) were cutting brambles for fencing in some low scrub not far from Bageetand bungalow about midday. One of these fancied he heard a low cry from the direction in which his fellows were working. He called to him several times, and, receiving no response, he and his fellow *gola* went in search of their comrade, when they saw a large tiger carrying off the man. They at once raised a shout and bolted to Koderma to inform the European residents there. Several gentlemen and a gang of coolies searched the locality, and in a dry water-course they found the body of the *gola*, one thigh and all the lower part of the belly having already been eaten. The tiger had seized the man by the back of the neck, so that death must have been almost instantaneous. Here to-day, ten miles away to-morrow, in the very opposite direction the next day, he held the borderland of the Hazaribagh and Gaya Districts in absolute terror so that the natives will not go about their usual avocations unless in large gangs, and even Europeans go armed when visiting their mining blocks. This brute has become more and more daring with each successive kill, and he has lately taken men from the middle of a gang. Very recently five natives were going along the forest road from Koderma to Rajowlee. The road winds through some low scrub before it enters the Reserved Forest of

Koderma. The fourth in the line of coolies was a man with a black umbrella over his head. His wife, with an infant child on her hip, was following. The foremost coolie fancied he saw something move behind a felled tree some distance ahead. He thought nothing more of the circumstance until he had passed the tree, when he heard a scream from the woman, who was standing in the middle of the road, with her child at her feet, shouting: "The tiger! The tiger! See! See!" There, sure enough, was the tiger carrying off the man with the umbrella, which he still grasped in his hand; the open umbrella catching in the brushwood and impeding the progress of the tiger. The men raised a shout, and moved a few paces in the direction of the brute, when it dropped its prey and turned on the men, snarling ferociously, which at once put them to flight. One of the men remarked that the tiger had lost its left ear and its eyesight appeared defective, as if it had been wounded by a charge of shot. It is of large size and of a light tawny colour. Hitherto it has baffled all the attempts of European and native *shikarees* to shoot it. So great has been the loss of human life, and so great the terror this man-eater has inspired in the neighbourhood, that it behoves the Government to take special measures to destroy it.

Jiban's tale was true as regards the peculiarities of this brute. At first he took to killing and eating only *golas*. Jiban says that it was because the *golas* always smell of cattle—a common food of tigers—and that this odour attracted him at first.

As *golas* grew more wary and kept out of his haunts, he tried a *chamar* or two. He has now taken to *agragrees* (iron smelters and charcoal-burners), and his last six kills have been among these men ; hence Jiban's appeal to me. Jiban's ideas of the power of the Government are great. By mere beat of drum the tiger can be debarred from slaying charcoal-burners. Apparently the report that this man-eater is of defective vision is correct, as only a few days ago, some coolies were returning from work at dusk, and one of the women had a bundle of wood on her head. The tiger sprang out of a thicket at the woman and seized the bundle of wood, with which he went crashing down the *khud*, growling ferociously the while. The coolies all bolted while the tiger was engaged with this novel prey, and no damage was done. One more instance of this brute's cunning. About six weeks ago a wood-cutter was engaged felling a *semul* tree within a hundred yards of the village of Pardiah. The time was about midday, and his wife usually took him a drink of water at this hour. On arrival at the tree she found only his axe, and noticed a few drops of blood on the ground. She raised an alarm, and the whole of the men employed at the mines turned out with drums, empty kerosine tins, spears, lathis, etc. All the European employés turned out also with guns. The whole of the forest near the village was beaten over, but no signs of the brute or his kill were found. Next day some vultures were seen alighting in a field in the immediate vicinity of the village. This was searched, and the poor victim's head, hands, and feet were found. The tiger had evidently taken the body among the tall corn-stalks and calmly devoured him while the beat was still going on in the forest.

TRAPPING A MAN–EATER FOR THE CALCUTTA ZOO.

MOST of those who travel by the East Indian Railway, know of Simultala as a picturesque little station at the head of the only *ghaut* along this otherwise almost dead level of a railway. From Gidhour to Simultala the line winds and twists over steep gradients among low hills covered with scrub forest, which stretch away north and south as far as the eye can see. From Monghyr on the north to Hazaribagh on the south, this belt of forest extends for more than two hundred miles. Its width is not much more than ten miles.

The scrub forest between Gidhour and Simultala is infested with tigers of the most dangerous type—man-eaters. More persons have been carried off and devoured by tigers between Gidhour and Simultala than in any other locality of similar size in all India. Mention is made of this tiger-infested tract in the Ain-i-Akbari, the revenue collectors of the Mogul Emperor Akbar being unable to collect the land tax for fear of man-eating tigers. Over three hundred persons are known to have been carried off by tigers in the country around Gidhour and Simultala during the last ten years. Skirting the densely populated and highly cultivated lands of South Behar, this forest is resorted to by the villagers for firewood, and while engaged in felling brushwood and tying it into bundles, they fall easy victims to the tigers that abound in this jungle. Last year no fewer than thirty-eight persons were devoured by one of these brutes, and so great was the terror he inspired that the woodcutters abandoned their calling, and the price of firewood went up several hundredfold in this neighbourhood. The villagers subscribed a sum of three hundred rupees and offered it as a reward for the destruction of this notorious man-eater. He was credited with abnormal powers. He was said to be many times the size of ordinary tigers and to be beautifully marked. He was also thought to be mad, as he would wantonly destroy cattle, killing five and six in a herd at one time. It is well known that tigers, as a rule, will kill one or at most two of a herd at one time, or just enough to last them for food for a week. It does not matter if the carcase becomes putrid, as apparently the tiger likes his meat "high." It is rare that the "kill" will last a week as vultures, jackals and crows devour all they can during the absence of the tiger. The Gidhour man-eater seemed to kill for the mere pleasure of killing, and on one occasion he destroyed in the afternoon four large milch buffaloes belonging to a small *zemindar*, but left their carcases untouched.

Human beings were his favourite food, and to get at his prey he has been known to stalk them for miles. Owing to his depredations, it was difficult to get cultivators to remain in the rice fields after dusk, so that much of the crops were destroyed at night by deer and pigs. The *zemindar* above alluded to, with considerable difficulty, managed to get a Kol and his wife from the Karagpur hills to watch his fields by night. A high platform on slender poles was erected in the centre of the field, and on this the Kol and his wife took up their quarters at dusk. The night being cold in winter, the pair had with them an earthen pot filled with fire and a supply of firewood to last the night. They had scarcely taken their places on the platform before a large tiger made his appearance, and walking up to the *machan* began sniffing round and round. Apparently he had not seen the couple, but had followed them up by scent, as he walked round and round the platform making larger circles in his hunt for the lost trail and repeatedly came back and sniffed at the poles of the frail edifice on which the pair were crouching in helpless terror. After a time he realised that his prey was on the platform above, and rearing himself on his hind legs he tried repeatedly to pull down the shaky fabric, but the slender poles gave him no foothold, so that he could not climb on to the structure, which was just beyond his reach. The hours went by, and time and again he renewed his efforts to pull down or climb the *machan*. The moon rose late and the occupants were in hopes that with the moon, the tiger would take his departure. The moon was in her zenith and the tiger had ceased his efforts for some time, which emboldened the Kol to peer over the edge of the platform, when the tiger rushed forward with a fierce snarl and redoubled his efforts to climb the poles. Reared on end, the tiger's head was within a few feet of the trembling pair, and they could feel and smell his hot fœtid breath as he snarled at the Kols above. Fearing that the structure would give way under the renewed efforts of the tiger, the man set about devising some means of getting rid of their dangerous assailant. His wife suggested that they should heat the piece of iron which forms the cutting part of a ploughshare which they had luckily taken up with them, and throw it on to the tiger's face when next he reared himself. The suggestion was good, and the fire was replenished with extra wood and blown to a brisk flame. Soon the iron was red hot, and when the tiger with open jaws again tried to claw them off their perch the Kol dropped the fuming metal straight into the gaping mouth of the tiger. With a fierce howl of rage and pain the tiger rushed away, and crouching down among some bushes, he kept groaning in pain and tried with his paws to soothe the burnt portion. This he kept up till late in the morning, and it was only when other cultivators arrived in a body to reap the corn that he went off into the forest. None of the native *shikarees* would venture into the forest to hunt this brute so great was their dread of his prowess. Even the few European sportsmen from Calcutta who tried to bag him failed in their efforts. The landlords were losing heavily, as not only was the royalty on firewood gone, but even the fields were neglected.

One day a mild-looking native called on the *zemindar* of Sheikpura who was a heavy loser by the depredations of the tiger, and offered to trap him, if he was given the promised reward. Eventually a bargain was struck that the man should get one hundred rupees, and that all expenses of constructing the trap should be borne by the villagers. The man disappeared for a day or two saying he was going to watch the tiger and find out its habits and the places it most frequented. On his return he asked that a ring fence, some twenty feet in diameter, of strong poles should be constructed at a point he indicated near a water-course. At one point the fence was open for about five feet and parallel walls of poles made a passage some thirty feet long, leading into the ring fence. Within the ring and near to the entrance he constructed a huge pit twelve feet long, eight feet wide and twelve feet deep. All the earth from this pit was carefully removed to some distance. Over the mouth of this pit he pegged down a cloth of sufficient size to cover it, and over this he strewed leaves. Beyond this pit and within the fence he securely fastened a buffalo to a stake, so that it could be plainly seen from the passage, but could not be got at, without crossing the pit. Before baiting his trap, he asked that no cattle should be allowed near the forest, and that the villagers should keep away, so that the tiger would be without food for some time. He then baited his trap with the live buffalo, and all went off till next day. It was found in the morning that a tiger had been round and round the trap, but had not entered the fence. The man was not disheartened. He said he was now certain of his foe, as the tiger was sure to come back if he did not kill elsewhere. A second night passed and the villagers again hastened to the trap, and there crouching in a corner of the pit was a tiger of the largest size, growling and snarling furiously at the sight of his human foes. In rushing to seize the buffalo he had to cross the pegged cloth, which gave way to his weight and hurled him into the pit. Immediately the joyful news went round, the villagers assembled in their thousands and made the forest ring with their shouts of exultation, and abuse of the tiger and his relatives for several generations. The magistrate was communicated with, and he thought the catch so good that the tiger ought to be sent to the Calcutta Zoo. There was no doubt it was the terrible man-eater, as the marks of the burn inflicted on it by the Kol were plainly visible.

The Zoo authorities sent up a portable cage on wheels. An inclined plane was cut leading from the exterior of the ring fence to the bottom of the pit and the cage, with door toward the pit, was gradually lowered. On nearing the pit the door was shut and the men from inside the cage cautiously worked through the bars until the intervening earth was removed. On the barrier of earth being removed, the tiger rushed furiously at the iron bars, but the stout iron resisted all his efforts. When all was ready the door was cautiously raised and the tiger hustled with long spears. He made for the open door, which was dropped on his entrance, and the famous Gidhour man-eater was now a close prisoner. Hundreds of willing hands took hold of the ropes attached to the cage and drew it amid resounding shouts to the surface. The old women and the village children assembled in crowds, and throwing pebbles at the tiger invited him to come now and eat them. "We will singe your whiskers and burn your tail, you coward," shouted they. This was kept up till the Gidhour station was reached, quite a multitude of persons joining the *cortège*, until the cage, with its contents, was safely entrained and on the way to Calcutta. Visitors to the Zoo at Alipore may still see this dreaded brute, a label on the cage giving the necessary information to identify him.

THE END.